Weakling
into
Warrior

Weakling into Warrior

Let the weak say, I am strong

Terence S. Benton

XULON PRESS

Xulon Press
2301 Lucien Way #415
Maitland, FL 32751
407.339.4217
www.xulonpress.com

© 2022 by Terence S. Benton

All rights reserved solely by the author. The author guarantees all contents are original and do not infringe upon the legal rights of any other person or work. No part of this book may be reproduced in any form without the permission of the author.

Due to the changing nature of the Internet, if there are any web addresses, links, or URLs included in this manuscript, these may have been altered and may no longer be accessible. The views and opinions shared in this book belong solely to the author and do not necessarily reflect those of the publisher. The publisher therefore disclaims responsibility for the views or opinions expressed within the work.

Unless otherwise indicated, Scripture quotations taken from the King James Version (KJV) – *public domain*.

Scripture quotations taken from the Holy Bible, New International Version (NIV). Copyright © 1973, 1978, 1984, 2011 by Biblica, Inc.™. Used by permission. All rights reserved.

Scripture quotations taken from the Holy Bible, New Living Translation (NLT). Copyright ©1996, 2004, 2007 by Tyndale House Foundation. Used by permission of Tyndale House Publishers, Inc.

Paperback ISBN-13: 978-1-66286-119-2
Ebook ISBN-13: 978-1-66286-120-8

Dedication

This book is dedicated to the memory of my Mother Trusynia S. Benton.

"Mom, you always wanted to finish writing your books and have them published. I know you would be extremely proud that I finished mine. You are one of my deepest inspirations. I love and miss you, Mommy!"

TABLE OF CONTENTS

Introduction..ix

Seek and submit 1
Addressing Weakness 29
Private Development............................ 45
The Discipline of Embarrassment 59
The Wisdom of Warfare 79
Emerge Strategically 119
Revenge.. 149
Wounded Warriors 173

Final Words.................................... 207
Acknowledgments 215
About the Author 217

Introduction

I like nonsense, it wakes up the brain cells. Fantasy is a necessary ingredient in living, it's a way of looking at life through the wrong end of a telescope. Which is what I do, and that enables you to laugh at life's realities.
—Dr. Seuss

The great storyteller Dr. Seuss compared fantasy to nonsense. He stated that fantasy wakes up the brain cells. Fantasy is a great escape from reality. Using fantasy, Dr. Suess was able to poke fun at reality. Looking at life through the wrong end of the telescope seems to create an illusion that the reality in front of his view was so much further away than it really is while looking at life through the correct side of the telescope brings reality closer.

Fantasy gives us an illusion of reality and within the realm of fantasy we can create the life that we fantasize about in the spaces that are not visible in reality. Fantasy does wake up the brain cells, but the brain cells should never reside in fantasy, because fantasy is dangerous when one's eyes are fixated on it. Fixating on fantasy can leave damaging effects. Fantasy is an escape from problems but never brings answers. The problem with fantasy is that when fantasies end the problems of reality become more aggressive. When reality becomes more aggressive, the need to escape to fantasy becomes greater. A person begins to live life in illusion and not intellect.

Many people live in fantasy to escape from reality, but they do not want to address the problems. Fantasy makes for a great story but not a great testimony. Fantasy can become reality when someone embraces it. But reality inevitably confronts fantasy, and reality creates problems that cannot be ignored. There is nothing wrong with imagination—God gave us imagination. But God gave us imagination so we can bring to life God given answers to life's problems, not as a permanent alternative to reality.

Some of us are more fixed on problems than they are fixed on solutions. Some of us are more interested in living in their fantasy world than letting God use them to touch the world. They have a weak perception of life. Many of us are more concerned about satisfying the world within us than reaching the world around us. I am guilty of letting fantasy be reality.

During the preparation for writing this book, I asked different people questions about books and reading to help me gather information for this book. My first question to each person I spoke with was do they read. Some of them read; some of them struggled with sitting down and cracking open a book. A lot of them said that they would read if they found a book that could really keep their attention. If they said that they really didn't read much or at all, I would stop asking them further questions.

The next question I asked the readers is whether they prefer fiction or nonfiction books. The word *fiction* means literature that describes imaginary events and people. Nonfiction is prose writing that is based on facts, real events, and real people, such as biography or history. Most of the people that I asked preferred fiction books over nonfiction. Only a few preferred nonfiction over fiction. After I asked them about what they preferred, I went into further conversation about why they preferred fiction or nonfiction.

Those few people who said they preferred nonfiction told me that it was because they loved learning new things about history and people. They applied the lessons that real-life people and events taught them. They were fascinated by history, biographies, and life instruction written or recorded by people who had a life message to convey. They loved gathering information and wisdom from real-life events. I am a nonfiction reader myself. I prefer nonfiction books over fiction, although I still like fiction books.

I learned that readers who love fiction love the escape that fiction books provide from daily life. Some fiction books teach valuable life lessons, but the authors teach the lessons through fictitious characters, life events, and story lines. Most fiction books have hidden messages that are not as upfront as nonfiction books. Fictional books take you on a journey in fantasy. The readers explained that fiction books provide a beautiful escape from life's pressures, troubles, and worries. Reading fiction provides them with an out-of-body experience of a fantasy world and of a life that is not their own.

Let me say that I have nothing against the reader who prefers fiction over nonfiction. I can kind of relate to them as a person who only used to read fictional books. I wasn't a reader at all. I can count on one hand how many books I've completed growing up, and they were fiction. I always loved to write but unfortunately, I got into reading as an adult. Reading provides that escape that we all are looking for. The relief from life's challenges and the ongoing story that unfolds before your eyes gives you a thrill that replaces the mundane feeling that daily life brings. A good fictional story adds spice to a dull moment and gives your mind a satisfying fantasy trip. Fictional stories are amazing and have their place, and while fictional stories are supposed to add spice to life's lessons, they are never supposed to be the meal. Jesus used parables or simple stories to illustrate a moral or spiritual lesson. His parables were teaching points for the true message. Jesus conveyed the truth He taught to His hearers by using the stories to break down the lessons that He taught.

Fictional stories are like the black pepper that you add to the chicken. The chicken represents the lesson. The chicken is the meal. You would never eat a bowl full of black pepper, because black pepper is a spice that is meant to season your food. Black pepper compliments the meal, it is not the meal itself. Black pepper can satisfy you for a moment, but it cannot give you substance.

It becomes a serious problem when fiction or fantasy stops being a relief and turns into a belief. When we accept a fantasy world as a real-life experience, we are trying to escape from reality to not deal with life. It's as though we desire a bowl of pepper because we don't feel like cooking the chicken. When we would rather read about, watch, and listen to gossip, drama, and horror through other characters' lives and experiences than deal with the gossip, drama, and horror in our own lives. Although we can learn from the characters we read about, we are not those characters. We are trying to change relief into belief by being more interested in solving the mysteries of others than addressing the mysteries we are confronted with.

I enjoy Marvel and DC Universe comic books and movies. As far as movies are concerned, I enjoy Marvel movies over DC Universe, and I really enjoy The Avengers and Spider-Man. I watch them often with my son and we are thrilled at the action-packed story lines every time. But it would be a true problem if I tried to live my life as Spider-Man. What if I woke up every morning and left my family to go fight crime as Spider-Man? Imagine if I went out into town with a Spider-Man costume attempting to stop crime and trying to climb buildings to protect the city as Spider-Man. You see how crazy the idea of a grown man with a family living in a fantasy as Spider-Man sounds, because these stories were created for enjoyment and not reenactment. You would probably think that I have a mental illness!

As strange as that sounds, as people we do it all the time. We entertain the fantasies, conspiracies, and fallacies of this society because we love the sense of escape that it brings. We have areas in our lives that lack substance that have never been addressed which leads us to a life of fantasy and falsehood. We run from addressing these places in our lives and in ourselves because we are afraid to finally deal with the life we have learned to escape. Our attempts to escape and not deal with the issues of life and the heart lead us to a life of fantasy. As we live in this fantasy, our problems pile up and our lives and emotions become even harder to manage.

Reality TV is a part of American culture that is also embraced around the world. Reality television is a view into the lives of celebrities—the rich, the famous—or people who desire to become all those things from exposing their lives on reality television. Reality television shows the personal business, conversation, and drama of people's lives. I have seen people embarrass themselves and their families for ratings. They fight, curse, yell, act like children all in the name of ratings. Drama keeps the viewers' attention. The highest rated reality television shows are those that are filled with cheating, fighting, gossip, and drama.

When I ask people why they love reality television so much, the response is simple, it's entertainment. Other people's scripted drama and gossip is entertaining to the viewer. What I realized is that although entertainment is an enjoyment, when it is used as a source of happiness, it becomes poison to the soul. People find an escape in entertainment and drama because it distracts them from their own personal dramas. Some people even take on the personalities of the dramatic characters that they watch and are entertained by. When entertainment becomes reenactment, it causes more damage to the soul because it is a make-believe world that gives us an escape from the problems in our lives that need to be handled and strengthens our personal problems against us.

Some people find their escape in strip clubs. Some find it in pornography. Some find their escape in perverted lifestyles and relationships. Some find their escape in sexual activities. Some find their escape in drinking and smoking. Some people find their escape in drugs. Some people find their escape in anger and rage. Some people find their escape by working nonstop. Some people find their escape in playing video games or watching television all day and night. Some people find their escape in locking themselves in their bedrooms and pushing others away. However, people find their escape, it will always cause catastrophic damage because we are not addressing the areas that we choose to hide from. We don't want to address the hatred in our hearts. We don't want to address the need to forgive a parent or family member. We don't want to address the rape, molestation, and sexual abuse. We don't want to address the physical, verbal, and mental abuse from a loved one, relative or a peer. We don't want to address the heartbreak, the distrust, and the anxiety that our past or present has caused. We might sometimes express it, but we don't always address it. Ignoring these areas causes us to believe the wrong things and live the wrong life.

We are more attracted to memorization than manifestation. We would rather hold on to our reliefs than let God work on our beliefs. We choose to live lives of make believe rather than let God construct our beliefs in life. We won't let God address these weak places in our lives because we love being distracted by fantasy. We hate dealing with reality. We let reality beat us to the ground because we don't let the Spirit of God manage the damage. We long for escape but we never learn to take the challenge of life and strike back! Biblically there is an answer! 1 Corinthians 10:13 tells us, "No temptation has overtaken you except what is common to mankind. And God is faithful; he will not let you be tempted beyond what you can bear. But when you are tempted, he will also provide a way out so that you can endure it."

We are tempted and tried in every aspect of life, but God is more faithful and consistent than are life's temptations. Only God can give a true way of escape from our trouble, not so you can run from it, but so you can bear it! God wants to give you the escape that leads to strength not weakness. He is the escape. God has given us tools to live and weapons to fight. But our mentalities must be transformed from weakness to spiritual strength. We must stop running from life and use the power that God has given us to deal with life and conquer it! We must learn to choose belief over relief. We must look beyond the surface and see purpose.

The only way that we can finally live the lives that we are purposed for is to be transformed into the people that God wants us to be. When we are living outside of what God has created us to be, we avoid the problems that God is using us to solve. Problems pile up when they are not dealt with. Even though we all have strengths, we also have weak areas that we won't let God address. These weak areas ruin every other area in our lives because we let them grow out of control. Sometimes we are so busy looking and judging everyone else's life and dealing with everyone else's problems that we don't allow God to address us. Weakness speaks through emotions; strength speaks through devotion.

God gave me this book to address the weakling in you. I know that it appears that you are strong, but there are some areas of your life that are out of control that you can't handle. These are weak areas that God wants to address. We usually fantasize in these areas. We usually build idols in idle places. Some of you might be muscular and strong on the outside, and you might have the confidence to get tasks done—to lead and to fight in certain areas—but we all have areas that make us feel like helpless children crying out for parental guidance and comfort. David was a leader and a great warrior, but he felt weak and ran from an enemy because of his loyalty. (I will explain this more in the book.) We all have areas where we feel weak. Some of us refuse to let God address these areas, but He wants to show you the warrior that you are in these areas so that these areas won't continue to spill over into every other part in your life. God wants the warrior that He has created you to be to take over every area of your life.

We are tempted and tried in every aspect of life, but God is more faithful and consistent than our temptations. God wants to give you the escape that leads to strength not weakness. He is the escape.

Jesus says this in Matthew 7:

> Why do you look at the speck of sawdust in your brother's eye and pay no attention to the plank in your own eye? How can you say to your brother, "Let me take the speck out of your eye," when all the time there is a plank in your own eye? You hypocrite, first take the plank out of your own eye, and then you will see clearly to

Introduction

remove the speck from your brother's eye. (Matthew 7:3–5)

I can relate. There were areas that I was strong and confident in. There were also areas of my life that reflected a weak and frail soul. This part of me began to spill over into every other part of my life because I refused to let God address it. When God addresses things, it disturbs our comfort. I wasn't willing for God to disturb the comfortability of my demise, so I ran from correction in these areas, but my problems eventually caught up with me and became catastrophic to my life and destiny.

God literally had to take me into isolation and work on my heart and manhood so that these weak areas would not take over my identity. God revealed to me my identity as a warrior so that I could fight against these weak areas in my life and not ignore them. I will explain the process of this experience later in the book. I want to share what I've learnt. Your story may differ from mine, but in some areas of your life you are weak, and this weakness holds back everything else in your life. I want to speak with you and to you in a place where you are pitiful and prideful. We all have those places. Usually in those places, pride resides. God hates pride. It exalts itself against God. Allow God to tear down your pride and address the weakness that you are attempting to cover up yourself.

God has called us to be warriors for His kingdom. When we refuse to let God address, correct, and strengthen us in those areas in our lives, we disqualify ourselves from the kingdom of God because we won't let God take control of our weaknesses. Observe these words of the Lord Jesus in Luke 9:62, "Jesus replied, 'No one who puts a hand to the plow and looks back is fit for service in the kingdom of God.'" Jesus was simply saying that those who are not ready to walk away from everything of their past and their life before they met Him are not fit to represent His kingdom and follow Him.

When we allow pride to cover our weaknesses instead of allowing God to address our weakness, it causes our weaknesses to become more aggressive. Our weaknesses obey our flesh. Our flesh is geared to rebel against God. Our mind, body, and spirit all are at constant war with our flesh. We are weak in places that are ruled by our flesh. We must deny our flesh and let God take control of the places where the weakness of flesh is in control. When we learn to live, we allow the Holy Spirit to take complete control of places where we are weak, and He will strengthen us to become the fearless kingdom warrior where we were once fearful earthly weaklings. Jesus says to His disciples "Watch and pray so that you will not fall into temptation. The spirit is willing, but the flesh is weak" (Matt. 26:41).

God has given me this book to address the weakling in us all. God has given me strategic steps for you and me to embrace transformation in these areas. God wants us to tear down our fantasies and so He can build up our destinies. God wants us to see manifestation in our lives.

INTRODUCTION

For us to see manifestation we must tear down idol memorization. We must allow God to address the weaknesses and not escape from them.

I'm going to give you a few transformative instructions which will give you steps to take so that you can embrace this transformation in your life. Apply them to your life, take notes and review them. I will be sharing with you some biblical wisdom and truths to teach you how God turns weaklings into warriors. There are many biblical accounts showing how God has strengthened weak people to become mighty and to do mighty acts, but for this book I've handpicked just a few to share with you to give you a specific picture that He wants me to share in this book. Take the steps of this book seriously. Pray about the instructions and information of this book. God is going to use this book to transform your life. Take this journey with me as God transforms us from weaklings to warriors.

I

SEEK AND SUBMIT

First Samuel 22 verses 1 and 2 are the passages of Scripture that the Holy Spirit drew my attention to concerning the subject of this book. I want us to review the passage together and then I will explain the lesson behind the passage that the Lord revealed to me. The Lord used these couple of verses to grab my attention for the formation of this book. Although these are not the only scriptures that will be mentioned and explained in this book, I would like to start with this passage, to lay the foundation of this subject. I want to explain two perspectives that I have received from this passage, two revelations of how God transforms weak people into mighty warriors. Let us read:

> David left Gath and escaped to the cave of Adullam. When his brothers and his father's household heard about it, they went down to him there. All those who

were in distress or in debt or discontented gathered around him, and he became their commander. About four hundred men were with him. (1 Samuel 22:1, 2)

Amen to the Word of God. It is light and life. I want us to peer into this passage of scripture carefully. I understand that these are only a few scriptures with few details, so allow me to explain the backstory for your understanding.

Let us first answer this question, why is David hiding in a cave? I have an answer, David is hiding from King Saul. King Saul was the king of Israel during David's time in biblical history (1020 to 1000 BCE.). King Saul was anointed to be king by the prophet Samuel. God rejected King Saul as king during his reign because of King Saul's disobedience (1 Sam. 15). In 1 Samuel 16 God used prophet Samuel to anoint David, the shepherd boy, the son of Jesse, to be the new king of Israel.

In the later part of 1 Samuel 16, King Saul was being tormented mentally by an evil spirit allowed by God because of King Saul's disobedience. King Saul requested a musician to play music for him to make him feel better. One of the servants requested David. David came to play for King Saul and the evil spirit left King Saul as David played. King Saul loved David so much that he made David his armor bearer. An armor bearer was responsible for carrying the king's fighting armor to battles and on military campaigns. In 1 Samuel 17, David delivers food to his brothers in battle and kills Goliath in the name of the Lord.

In 1 Samuel 18, King Saul begins appointing David over armies and sends David on warfare missions. King Saul also grows fearful of David because He sees that God is with David. King Saul feels jealous of David because David was being praised by the people over Saul (1 Sam. 18:6–8) and even tries to kill David after God allows an evil spirit to take over King Saul. David at the time was Saul's personal minister of music and leader of King Saul's troops. Saul's son, David's best friend, cautioned David that King Saul wanted to kill David and sets up a plot to help David escape Saul's murder attempt (1 Sam. 20). Saul wanted to kill David because he was afraid of David and would not accept that David was anointed by God over him. King Saul hated the fact that David was being elevated by God and exalted by the people.

We journey into 1 Samuel 21 where David is on the run from Saul. David went to the city of Nob and met with Ahimelek the priest. The priest gave him food and a sword, the sword David used to kill Goliath. David left Nob and went to the Philistine city of Gath to find refuge. This is a very important detail, because the Philistines are adversaries of Israel. David was on the run from the king that he was actively serving. David was torn.

While in Gath, David attempted to talk with Achish, the King of Gath. While attempting to meet with Achish,

Achish's servants noticed David was one of Saul's servants (1 Sam. 21:11) David took this very seriously and created a diversion to cover up his identity. David began pulsating and allowing saliva to run down his beard. David used wisdom and he began to act like a lunatic so that he would cover up his identity. This made Achish question why his servants would bring a lunatic into his presence (1 Sam. 21:12–14). David left Nob and went into hiding.

So, we approach chapter 22 with the backstory of why David was hiding in the cave of Adullam. David hid himself in the cave because he was on the run for his life. As we read further into 1 Samuel 22:1, we see that David's brothers and father's household heard that David was hiding in the cave, so they went down to the cave to dwell with David while David was in hiding. This verse is one of the perspectives that I would like to bring out in this book. The perspective of how people flocked to David while he was in hiding. God was transforming David, shifting his mindset from running from kingdoms to running a kingdom.

Another key verse and perspective that I would like to bring out is 1 Samuel 22:2. I am going to explain the two perspectives during this chapter because it really paints the picture of God's process of transformation. These two perspectives from the two scriptures are the very foundation of how God transforms the weak into warriors. I purposely keep injecting 1 Samuel 22:2 to this passage because I want to thoroughly break it down.

First Samuel 22:2 talks about a clan of people who were distressed, indebted, and discontented who came to be with David while he was in hiding. These people gathered around David and made David their commander. About 400 hundred men came and followed David.

We see the two viewpoints of transformation. From one viewpoint we see how God transformed a runner into a leader. We see another viewpoint of God originated the transformation of a despaired clan into a distinguished army. Let's take a deeper look into the first perspective for insight on how God took David, who was weak at the time, and chose him to lead a clan while he was on the run from King Saul.

The Transformation of David

In 1 Samuel 22:1 David is hiding King Saul in the cave of Adullam from because King Saul wants to kill him. We can only imagine the amount of horror that David is dealing with. David is loyal to King Saul. Up until the time that David found out that King Saul wanted to kill him, he fought for King Saul's army and even led the troops. Out of his honor for King Saul, David refused to believe that King Saul wanted to kill him. When it was finally confirmed that King Saul wanted to kill David, David ran into hiding, confused and emotional.

Amid David's distress, agony, and paranoia, God led David's family to him for him to lead (1 Sam. 22:1). David was broken, betrayed, and fearful, but God still chose David to take the lead. David's family flocked to David for security, while David was insecure. Again, 1 Samuel 22:2 says, "All those who were in distress or in debt or discontented gathered around him, and he became their commander. About four hundred men were with him."

Along with David's family, 400 people flocked to David for security and training. God allowed David to gain a clan to lead during his suffering. David received a following while he was on the run. David was tasked with hiding and leading at the same time. The scripture says that those who were in distress, in debt, and discontented gathered around David and he became their commander (1 Sam. 22:2). David grew into command while his life was on demand. David was now burdened with leading and training weak people, while he was weak himself. David had to train while in pain. David had to strengthen weak people into an army, even while he needed strength himself. How could this be? Why did God allow David to lead while in hiding?

The first reason that God used David to lead in hiding was to show David how it felt to rule a kingdom as a king. David was anointed king by the prophet Samuel when he was younger but did not become king right away. Notice that throughout the Bible narrative God never calls someone to do something extraordinary without testing their faith and character for what He called them to accomplish. Testing is a very important component in growing into our God-given purpose. God allowed King Saul to grow a hatred for David to put David in a place of testing. God already approved David, but now God wanted to prove David.

David ran into the cave of Adullam for a resting place, but God used the cave as a testing place. God showed David how to rule a kingdom from a cave. David established a village while he was displaced. God was giving David the true heart of a king while David was running from a king. David went from being a shepherd boy with a flock of sheep, to leading King Saul's troops, to leading a clan of his own. With all three of these times of shepherding, God was proving David's heart, transforming him from caveman to a kingdom man. God upgraded David from being rejected to being respected.

The cave was the perfect place for God to transform David. Although David was a warrior in King Saul's army, God had to transform his mentality in the cave. David had a vulnerable mentality. God gave David a valuable mentality. David had areas that needed to be transformed from weak into warrior for him to make warriors out of the weak among him. Leading and transforming the clan was not just a responsibility for David but an opportunity for David. In David's insecurity, David's newly trained warriors would be David's security and God's assurance of His selection of David to be king of Israel.

The Transformation of the 400

Again, 1 Samuel 22:2 says, "All those who were in distress or in debt or discontented gathered around him, and he became their commander. About four hundred men were with him."

I want to give you the second perspective of transformation by explaining how God transformed the 400 weaklings in David's clan into mighty warriors using David's command. David was tasked with transforming these weak people into strong warriors.

The 400 flocked to David in desperate need of training, correction, and protection. These distressed, indebted, and discontented clansmen were led to David because, just like David, they were on the run for their lives. Some of the 400 owed money and were running from harsh masters. Some of the 400 were being tormented by the Philistines and other gentiles who invaded and ransacked their homes. Some of the 400 were sick. Some were discontented from the leadership of King Saul. All these people flocked to David for refuge. The 400 were refugees. The 400 gathered to David for hope. God led the 400 to David while David was in the cave, and the cave became a private training ground for the 400. God uses hiding places as tools of development.

Transformation can only take place in a private place. Look at seeds in the ground when they are planted. They can only grow if they are buried in dirt. Also, like a caterpillar in a chrysalis. Development works best in a dark place. Development can only take place in a setting that is undisturbed. Privacy is a place of undivided attention on the target areas of development. In the cave, David could properly train the weaklings and focus on their development, while the weaklings focused on the training. It was up to David to train them, and up to the 400 to embrace the training.

Submit to the Training and to the Trainer

Now that we have explained the story of David and the 400, I want to give practical and applicable wisdom to those who God has called on this transformation journey. The coming chapters will be God-given wisdom and steps to take to embrace the transformation from weakling to warrior. Apply these steps, let the process begin and continue.

The weak and distressed people recognized that David was a strong leader—even in his distress—they recognized that they needed David's leadership and training. The 400 submitted to David in the state that they were in. One of the most important parts of training and overcoming weakness is that you submit to training, to every aspect of training. More importantly, you must allow the Spirit of God to lead you to a trainer. You must find a commander and submit to their command. It's important to submit to the trainer as well as to the training. Once you lock into your commander, and humble yourself to training, the development will take place.

When a person needs assistance with their physical fitness goals, they seek a knowledgeable personal trainer to help them to reach the fitness goals. The personal trainer sets time aside to personally teach and train the trainee so that they can start working towards the results that the trainee desires. The personal trainer is responsible for stretches, exercise, diet regimens and the accountability of the person or people they are training. When the person who desires to be trained submits to the trainer and the training techniques and challenges, the desired results manifest because of the person's submission to the trainer and training. The trainer might tell them to stop eating certain foods or eating after a certain time, teach them new exercises, or even make them reach for greater fitness goals. If the trainee is serious about results, they will submit to the voice of the trainer and the lifestyle of the training.

David was now responsible for the wellbeing and development of weak wannabe warriors. David was now tasked with showing them the tactics, disciplines, diet, mentality, and lifestyle of true warriors. It was up to the weak clansmen to submit. Submission brings transmission and transmission brings transformation. God is doing the same thing for you in this transformative season of your life. God is teaching you the appetite and lifestyle of a warrior. You must fully embrace and submit to the trainer's voice and the training course.

Also, my fellow saints, shift your mindset from believing that you must be healed before you can answer the call of discipleship. The Lord will heal you as you follow His instructions. God doesn't base your training on how weak you are. God bases your training on how strong He is. Don't worry about your condition. There is a conditioning in the calling of God. Just come and be healed.

The Commission of Discipleship

Psalm 34, which was written by David in the cave of Adullam, is not only a declaration of David's faith in God but also the invitation for training to the group of 400 distressed people who came to David. Psalm 34 is an invitation to discipleship and training. David was giving the crowd hope in God and a promise to train and lead them in the ways of God.

Psalm 34 reads in part, "Come all ye children, listen to me, I will teach you the fear of the Lord" (Ps. 34:11 KJV). David was talking to the 400 in this verse where he is putting out a call of discipleship to the 400. This was more than David's invitation to the 400 to submit to his training. This was a call of submission. David realized that although some of the 400 were adults, they needed to be trained like children; they needed to be raised again. David not only invites the 400 hundred to submit to his commands, but he committed himself to teach the 400 the fear of the Lord. If David could establish that he trained them in the fear of the Lord, the 400 would be easier to train because the fear of the Lord would be the core of training.

Fear of the Lord is not about being scared of God but about how to have true reverence for God. David committed to teach them how to reverence the Lord God in all their ways, so that they could be successful in doing what God had called them to do. True reverence of God in every aspect of life produces excellence in every aspect of life. Fear of the Lord produces pure godly works. Reverence produces excellence.

The fear of the Lord also gives us insight and knowledge which is key in training. Proverbs 1:7 says "The fear of the Lord is the beginning of knowledge, but the fool despises wisdom and instruction." A fearless warrior without fear of their enemies is a great warrior, but a fearless warrior without fear of the Lord is a foolish warrior. The fear of the Lord gives us the very heart of God as we reverence and honor God. All our ways will honor God when we learn how to honor God during development. It is also important that your commander fears the Lord God and is committed to helping you revere the Lord God during the development process.

In 2019 I became a deputy sheriff. For privacy reasons I will not mention the city where I became a deputy sheriff. While I was in the sheriff's academy, my instructors drilled into our class the importance of upholding the core values and beliefs of the sheriff's office. The more that they were able to drill the beliefs and values into our mentalities, the more they could shape us to become great deputies because the instilling of the organization's values and beliefs gave us a "why" factor in training. We were taught to understand why we do what we do as deputy sheriffs and why we should be honored to do it. They taught us to hold high the name of the Sheriff's Office and the badge that we carried. It taught us reverence for the office that we'd taken an oath to uphold.

This is the same lesson that David was inviting the clan of weaklings to believe. David was teaching that their core beliefs and values were based upon their reverence for God. If David could shift their focus from their own abilities to the abilities of God, he could train them without the limitation of who they thought they were and put it on who God is. Allow God to lead you to a leader who will teach you to fear Him. Allow God to train you through the teacher He has given you to show you how to truly reverence Him.

Submit to your commander no matter what state they are in when you find them. The 400 found David hiding in a cave and they were willing to hide with him just to be with him. David was in a terrible state at the time, but the 400 still submitted to his leadership. David was confused, conflicted, afflicted, and paranoid, but the 400 still decided to submit to his training. The 400 found David in hopelessness and fragility, but they were still in need of David's training.

Don't forsake the lesson of the teacher God has led you to because you catch them in their own battle. Embrace and submit to your God-appointed teacher based on how well they are handling their own battle. Watch their techniques; study their attitude and temperament. Whether good or bad, learn the lessons that God is teaching you through them. Submit to them if they have the grace of God to teach you the lesson.

The 400 had a testimony of David's anointing to train. As mentioned before, David was in many battles and was the leader of King Saul's army. David was known for training the best warriors. The 400 were after David's ability to whip them into shape. They sought after David and submitted to him.

David was anointed to gather the scattered. David was shepherd of his father's flocks and grew to lead and train King Saul's troops. David was anointed and appointed to scattered people and flocks and to pull them together. He trained scattered people and transformed them into gathered people. The 400 knew that they were in the right hands, so they submitted to David in a rough place.

Let's examine the stories of the Son of God, Christ Jesus, choosing his disciples. Let us investigate Matthew 8:18–22. I want to show you how this passage of New Testament scripture relates to the story of David and the 400 in 1 Samuel 22. Let us read about our Lord and learn a lesson about what it takes to submit to true leadership. Let's read Matthew together:

> When Jesus saw the crowd around him, he gave orders to cross to the other side of the lake. Then a teacher of the law came to him and said, "Teacher, I will follow you wherever you go." Jesus replied, "Foxes have dens and birds have nests, but the Son of Man has no place to lay his head." Another disciple said to him, "Lord, first let me go and bury my father. But Jesus told him, "Follow me, and let the dead to bury their own dead." (Matthew 8:18–22 NIV)

Amen to the Word of God! This delightful passage of sacred scripture is the core of this part of the lesson about submission. No matter the condition or the position of the teacher, be ready to follow, whether in a cave or palace, be ready to submit.

Just like David in 1 Samuel 22, Jesus was displaced. Jesus did not have an earthly residence although the earth was already His. David's life experiences resembled the life of Christ very closely. If you read the genealogy of Jesus in Matthew 1, you will discover that Jesus is in the lineage of David, through Joseph, His earthly father. Jesus was also being sought out by His enemies. The Pharisees,

Sadducees, and teachers of law were committed to get rid of Christ Jesus. Jesus was not on the run for His own life, He was on the run to bring the lives of His creation back to the Father. Just as David had with his flock, Jesus gathered the scattered. Jesus was hated for restoring those who were deemed unworthy. Jesus would often go into hiding away from those who wanted to get rid of him. Jesus was a challenge and a threat to the religious leaders and officials of that day because they were hoping for a Messiah who would overthrow the powers of the Roman Empire and give Israel complete power over all the nations. Jesus didn't fit that description because He lived His life as a common man. Though He lived as a common He did miracles and explained the kingdom of God like the Messiah. His enemies hated Him for making Himself equal with God and explaining the law without their approval, which He did not need. Jesus was not weak like David; Jesus didn't need to be transformed like David. Jesus was and is living breathing transformation. Jesus is the strength. Jesus displayed transformation everywhere He set His foot. Jesus embodied the fear of the Lord even as He was Himself the Lord that should be feared.

Let's examine verse 19 of Matthew 8 more closely. We see the teacher of the law attempting to follow Christ Jesus. The teacher sought out Christ for reasons unknown to make Jesus His commander. Christ gave him the conditions of following in verse 20 "Foxes have dens and birds have nests, but the Son of Man has no place to lay his head." Jesus's condition and position at the time was to be without residence so that He could travel with His followers and bring salvation.

The cost of following Jesus at the time was complete acceptance of Christ's conditions at the time and submitting to His position. We must count the cost of following Christ and choose to commit to the cost. Those who commit to the cost are true followers. True disciples don't mind following a traveler, like David and Christ Jesus were. They will run behind the runner to receive their discipline. True disciples chase chastisement and chastisers.

Look again at what Christ told a disciple in verses 21 and 22: "Another disciple said to him, 'Lord, first let me go and bury my father.' But Jesus told him, 'Follow me, and let the dead bury their own dead.'" Some would think that verse 22 was a very bold and inconsiderate statement for Christ Jesus to say to a man with a dying father. Although it was a strong condition, Jesus knew that following Him was more important than handling personal affairs. Quite frankly, when we follow Jesus Christ, He will take care of all our personal affairs as we take care of what He's instructed us to do in His kingdom.

Honestly, if this disciple really believed in Christ and wanted to follow, he would soon find out that he was the disciple of the Resurrection Himself. Jesus is the Resurrection (John 11:25). Jesus was able to heal the disciple's dying father. This speaks the truth that if we commit to the command of Christ, He will take command and take care of our lives.

Second Timothy says, "Join with me in suffering, like a good soldier of Christ Jesus. No one serving as a soldier gets entangled in civilian affairs, but rather tries to please his commanding office" (2 Tim. 2:3–4 NIV). Apostle Paul writes this to Timothy, his son in the gospel, encouraging Timothy to continue God's work even in suffering. These New Testament scriptures also remind us that when we enlist into God's kingdom as warriors, no matter how weak we think we are, the affairs of the world are not the main objective anymore. Now the objective is to please the commander, and as our commander God will take care of us.

In this development process it's of extreme importance that we walk away from everything to submit to the commander and His command. I urge you to be led by the Holy Spirit and study who you are to submit to as your commander. Whoever the Spirit leads you to means that Christ is with them, so when you submit to them, you submit to Christ. Paul sums this up in 1 Corinthians chapter 11 where he says, "Follow my example, as I follow the example of Christ" (1 Cor. 11:1 NIV).

When The Holy Spirit leads you to a commander, seek them out and submit to them so that God can use their training to develop the inner warrior in you.

The Call of Discipleship

One does not choose to be a disciple; one is chosen to be a disciple. A person may be chosen for discipleship, but that person has the option to choose whether or not he will follow the call of discipleship. The call of discipleship is an invitation from an instructor to walk closely with the instructors. Discipleship is intimate. Discipleship is a call to strangers to become familiar with the voice of the instructor and the life of instructions. Discipleship is a call to eat at the teacher's table. A call of discipleship is a call to close communion. God is calling you into close quarters with Him. God uses instructors to impart transformational lessons into disciples. The Lord is calling you to the table, will you choose to answer?

Christ is seen often in the New Testament sharing meals with His disciples, telling them secrets of the kingdom, and training them to do kingdom work. Christ thoroughly explained that there was a cost to discipleship. In Luke 14 Jesus talks about the call to discipleship by using a parable about a rich man who prepared a great banquet for his guests, but people were too busy to come and feast with him:

> When one of those at the table with him heard this, he said to Jesus, "Blessed is the one who will eat at the feast in the kingdom of God." Jesus replied: "A certain

man was preparing a great banquet and invited many guests. At the time of the banquet he sent his servant to tell those who had been invited, 'Come, for everything is now ready.' "But they all alike began to make excuses. The first said, 'I have just bought a field, and I must go and see it. Please excuse me.' "Another said, 'I have just bought five yoke of oxen, and I'm on my way to try them out. Please excuse me.' "Still another said, 'I just got married, so I can't come.' "The servant came back and reported this to his master. Then the owner of the house became angry and ordered his servant, 'Go out quickly into the streets and alleys of the town and bring in the poor, the crippled, the blind and the lame.' "'Sir,' the servant said, 'what you ordered has been done, but there is still room.' "Then the master told his servant, 'Go out to the roads and country lanes and compel them to come in, so that my house will be full. I tell you, not one of those who were invited will get a taste of my banquet.'" (Luke 14:15–25 NIV)

It is important that we understand the meaning of this parable. The man preparing the great banquet sent out the call to all those he had chosen to feast with at the banquet. The party guests who were invited made excuses on why they chose not to attend. The man began to get angry and sent his servant to welcome the disabled and the poor to the feast. After the servant obeyed, there was still room in the banquet for more guests. The man commanded that his servant go to the roads and highways sending the call out for the feast so that the banquet can be filled.

The Lord is calling for those who will hear His voice and call to follow Him. As we see, people are often too busy with their earthly affairs to answer the call, but they want to reap the benefits of communion with God. No call, no communion. The call is open, it's up to a person to hear the call and to answer it. The call to discipleship is not for the busy. The call of discipleship is for the hungry who are in need of communion. Jesus states in Matthew 5: "Blessed are those who hunger and thirst for God's approval. They will be satisfied" (Matt. 5:6 GW). When you hunger for God's instruction, the Lord will satisfy you with wholeness. He will commune with you. You will be satisfied when you choose communion with God. You will be whole with Him.

Matthew 22:1–14 mirrors Luke 14:15:24 except it adds to the story. The certain man that Luke 14 talks about is described as a king preparing a wedding banquet for his son. Also, Luke tells about a man who showed up without wedding attire for the banquet. The man was tied up by the hands and feet and thrown outside into darkness. Verse 24 of Luke 14 describes the key in discipleship where it says, "For many are invited, but few are chosen."

Many are invited to discipleship, but only a few answer the call. Only few hear the call because many are too busy to accept the call. Discipleship is a denial, a canceling of plans. Discipleship is a divorce from our daily busyness and a commitment to progress. Progression in the kingdom is the hunger of discipleship, which proclaims, "I want to eat." Walking intimately with the instructor is the communion of discipleship, which proclaims, "let us eat." It is a good position to be invited, it's an even greater position to choose to come.

The Communion of Discipleship

"Few are willing to unlearn and relearn in submission to discipleship." —Prophet Richard Rowe

To further break down the words of my brother Prophet Rowe, few are willing to forget all that they know to follow Christ's commands. Many are busy in ministry but disobedient to Christ. Many are busy in ministry but not progressing in the kingdom. They are not willing to unlearn toxic religious behaviors and toxic human behaviors to embrace the commands and freedom of Christ. This becomes a place of pride against God because a person will exalt their own knowledge over the commands and call of Christ.

In Christianity, especially in the western world, we are taught to follow the church that we gather with rather than the Christ in whose name the church gathers. We are taught to seek to please people and not to seek to please God. We are taught about church doctrine and the vision of the church, rather than being taught the gospel of Jesus Christ and sound doctrine. We can be in church for so long and still not know Christ. We become religiously committed to the church but forsake being relationally devoted to Christ. But the church is the body of Christ, and Christ is the head. We often take pride in being the body, but we forsake submitting to the head. Some sit as members of churches for many years and still don't understand Jesus, the gospel, the Holy Spirit, and how to bear good fruit. Somehow, we are taught that our dedication to our church automatically qualifies us as good Christians, even if we are not submitted to Christ Himself. We know the religion about God but don't personally know the God of the religion.

God wants us to know Him personally, not just religiously. Anyone can be religious, even sinners. God requires heart connection. God wants to be our Father and our friend, not just our creator. When God created male and female, He walked and talked with them as a Father and friend, not just as the Creator. Although mankind turns their back on God's Fatherhood through the curse of sin, through Christ Jesus, men are reconciled back to the Father as new creatures and children. Christ is the garden where mankind and God dwell together.

Many religious people live disciplined lives according to their religion and still stand in disobedience to God because they refuse to allow Christ to teach them the way. They are too prideful about their own beliefs and self-righteousness to bow down to the call of Christ. Even some of us who are churchgoers are not willing to unlearn what they heard about Christ to hear from Christ for ourselves. Many don't really know Christ. Many people are going to church but have not accepted the call of Christ. They feel that their commitment to the local church is equated to their commitment to Christ. Although fellowship with the church is important, knowing of God and knowing God are two different positions. There are many high-ranking church leaders who don't know Christ for themselves; they just know ministry. Although God uses them, and people really are blessed by their gift, they don't know Christ in their hearts and have not committed their hearts to following Christ. Christ addresses such people in Matthew 7, which reads:

> "Not everyone who says to me, 'Lord, Lord,' will enter the kingdom of heaven, but only the one who does the will of my Father who is in heaven. On that day many will say to me, 'Lord, Lord, did we not prophesy in your name, and cast out demons in your

name, and do many mighty works in your name?' And then will I declare to them, 'I never knew you; depart from me, you workers of lawlessness.' (Matthew 7:21–23 author's paraphrase)

Outside of church, some people will dedicate themselves to anything else but to follow Christ. Many aren't willing to give it all up to follow Jesus. Many will give up their lifestyle to go into the military, go to college, start a job, join a gang, or even begin practicing other religions before they give up everything to follow Christ. This is because the flesh refuses to bow to Christ , the Word of God (Rom. 8:7). It seems so much easier to commit to everything else which causes drastic adjustments in our lives than to submit to Christ whose way is easier to follow. Jesus says this in Matthew 11: "Come to me, all you who are weary and burdened, and I will give you rest. Take my yoke upon you and learn from me, for I am gentle and humble in heart, and you will find rest for your souls. For my yoke is easy and my burden is light" (Matt. 11:28–30 NIV).

There is an aspect of fellowship in the following. We are not followers if we are not fellowshipping. It is possible to follow things of God without committing to the God of the things. Discipleship is a constant surrendering, following, and fellowship with the Lord. Surrender to discipleship.

One of my favorite movie series is a martial arts movie series called Ip Man. It is a four movie series about the life of a grand master of the martial art of Wing Chun, his fighting style, his fighting adventures, and how he trained famous martial artist Bruce Lee. In the movie installment *Ip Man 2*, Master Ip (Ip Man) puts out flyers around Hong Kong about a Wing Chun school that he was planning to open. Master Ip was a Wing Chun grandmaster and was sending out a call for disciples. After a period of time, one interested young man came to Master Ip's house to check out the school. The young man challenged Master Ip to a fighting match to prove his fighting skills. He agreed that if Master Ip won, he would pay fees to Master Ip's school, and Master Ip agreed. Master Ip twisted the young inquirer like a pretzel using his superior Wing Chun skills. Instead of paying the fees to Master Ip's school for losing, the young man ran off and grabbed three of his friends to fight Master Ip. Master Ip asked them to leave, but they challenged him to a fight—Master Ip versus all three of the young man's friends—Master Ip accepted. Master Ip twisted all three guys with his fighting skill and beat all three men. After Master Ip beat them, he asked them to leave. The first young man in the initial fight bowed and asked Master Ip to accept him as a student. The young man's friends followed him and bowed and asked to be accepted as disciples as well. Master Ip accepted them.

I brought this story up to show that Master Ip was not responsible for the answer of the students who would follow him. He was responsible for putting out the call. The young men became disciples when they decided to surrender to the call. Just like Jesus showed the disciples a miracle when he told them to follow Him, Master Ip showed his students his wonderful fighting skills and confirmed the call to show that he was worthy enough to follow. It was up to the disciples to leave what they knew and follow the instructor.

It's up to us to leave all that we know and follow our instructor, Jesus Christ, and who He has drawn us to for training.

II

Addressing Weakness

Let's go back to the original story. Again, 1 Samuel 22:2 states. "All those who were in distress or in debt or discontented gathered around him, and he became their commander. About four hundred men were with him."

This verse of scripture expressed the state that the clan of 400 despaired people were in when they gathered to David. Although he was in a despaired state himself, the expression of the physical and emotional state of the 400 was greater. The 400 distressed, indebted, and discontented people were living in the expression of weakness as a lifestyle. David would have to address this lifestyle of weakness to strengthen this group into what God had sent them to be. David would have to help the 400 destroy the mindset of living their expression of weakness as a lifestyle. David had to challenge the 400 to shift their expression from an expressed weakness into an addressed weakness. Once David addressed their expression of weakness, he was able to transform that weakness into an expressed strength.

Just like the 400, we all have or have had expressions of weakness that we have embraced as a lifestyle. For those who still have a lifestyle of expressed weakness, we must allow God to address those areas and break the lifestyle. Areas of weakness in our lives that are not addressed are used by the enemy to sabotage every moment of purpose that God has designed us to have.

Our lifestyle of expressed weakness causes us to live below the bar that God has set in our lives. Situations and traumas have caused us to have areas of weakness that we have now embraced as a lifestyle. We feel that we now must live with these weaknesses because the weakness will never go away when, truth be told, these areas of weakness have not been addressed.

We have made lifestyles out of the weak places in our lives. These weak places give us a false sense of freedom or "fantasies." The false sense of freedom tells us that we are free to give in to our weaknesses without any consequences, when really you are a slave to your weaknesses and now live a lifestyle of expressed weakness.

Let me explain what I mean by a lifestyle of "expressed weakness." A lifestyle of expressed weakness is a life that we choose to live that gives us a disposition of being identified with what we struggle with. Expressed weakness is a choice to accept our weakness as a character trait. Those who live the life of expressed weakness have embraced the enslavement of their struggle and have set up a perimeter in their lives to support their expression.

Some of us have suffered very traumatizing circumstances in life that have caused underdeveloped areas in our lives. These are areas that are still sensitive where we are still vulnerable. These are areas that we still cry and get sad about that make us act out of character or act in rage. These are areas that we disguise with pride.

Some of these weak areas have become our character. Often, our habits and addictions are centered on the weaknesses that we have. Some people deal with lifestyles of sin and rebellion because of these areas of weakness. Some of us have sexual perversions and addictions because of these areas of weakness. Some of us have alcohol and drug problems because of the weakness or weaknesses. Some of us compare ourselves to others and have low self-esteem. Some of us hold hatred and remorse in our hearts. Some of us deal with having a nasty attitude. Some of us deal with depression and anxiety because of these areas of weakness. Some of us deal with financial problems and bad decision-making. Some of us deal with laziness and procrastination. Some of us deal with relationship, friendship, family, and marital problems because of these weaknesses. Some of us deal with suicidal thoughts. All of these come from a place of unaddressed weakness.

David had the task of developing his clan by addressing their expression of weakness. David had to end their expression. He had to transform their self-view from a place of expressed weakness to a place of addressed weakness. He was tasked with showing the 400 how to allow God to use their weaknesses to fuel the purpose that God had for them. David had to use an initial shock to shatter the self-view that the clan had of themselves.

In this secluded place David had to break down the clan's lifestyle of expressed weakness or fragile self-view and rebuild them into an addressed lifestyle of self-worth. David broke them down to take them from a state of vulnerability into a state of value. For David to raise their standard he had to break their standard and give them God's standard. David had to shock them out of their state. Every good training starts with initial shock.

Initial shock is something that suddenly happens which is unpleasant, upsetting, or very surprising at the beginning of a process. Any good trainer knows how important initial shock is in the beginning of the process of training. Initial shock is used by instructors to grab the attention of the trainee to challenge them and push them into a state of change. The initial shock process is the initiation process of breaking down self- and world-view.

The initial shock initiates a demolition of emotions, views, comfortability, and self-awareness. Initial shock shatters coping strategies and habits. Initial shock clears the floor for recreation. Initial shock is designed to push trainees to their limit, to break the limits that they have put on themselves, and to give them new limits to push.

God uses initial shock to wake up our ability. He destroys comfortability to bring out ability. The words *comfortability* and *vulnerability* have the word *ability* in them. God uses shock to destroy what's comfortable and vulnerable to let ability stand alone. Embrace the initial shock. Change your perspective about this uncomfortable process.

Don't focus on the shock, focus on the standard. God uses the shock to shift your self-view from an emotional state to a devotional state. God wants you to be devoted to the process. God uses initial shock to challenge how we think, to destroy it and build it back up. Embrace the shock. The shock is a strategy used for change.

In basic military training, instructors use initial shock to break down the trainees' civilian mindset. The instructors yell, taunt, and give far fetched instructions and expectations to recruits to break their mindsets and to rebuild their minds. The instructors break down basic civilians and build up military experts. Their goal is to bring stress. The stress that military training brings to the recruits not only stresses them but stretches them. Initial shock is vital in military training.

There is a plan in the pain. Although stress is involved, God is not stressing you, He is using the stress to stretch you beyond who you think you are. God wants to destroy who you think you are and build who He has designed you to be. God is using the shock to bring strategies to an underdeveloped area. He is using stress to address you. It is important to God to destroy your lifestyle of expressed weakness. He is allowing stress to stretch your weakness to strength and to bring restoration to a damaged place. God is stretching, while life is stressing you.

Whether we allow the stress to turn into distress is up to us. God does not want the stress to turn us to a mentality of distress but a mentality of progress. When you are locked on the lesson more than the stress, distress is not an option. We can either let the stress stretch us or oppress us. Press through the stress and you will be stretched.

God displayed through giving David's responsibility for the 400 that He wants to transform our damaged places into managed places. God used David to turn damaged people into managed people by addressing their issues and training them to manage their damage. God's will for us is that we be diligent managers of our lives. We must be trained to manage the skills, ability, and responsibilities that God has purposed for us. We must allow these weak areas to be addressed, tear down our perspective about them, and be taught to manage ourselves according to God's will.

How Addressing Weakness Transformed Gideon

For this section of chapter 2, I want to backtrack to a passage of scripture in the book of Judges. The book of Judges was written by the prophet Samuel who also wrote the book of 1 Samuel up unto the point of his death, after which another author wrote the rest of the story. Prophet Samuel authored other books of the Old Testament, but I will not name them so that I can bring out this next point. My goal is to show how God addresses weak areas in those He has called to do great things. First, let me give you the backstory of Judges 6. I will stop at a certain part of this passage and explain valuable points and revelations given to me about this passage of scripture.

Judges 6 starts with the explanation of how the Israelites continued to do evil things in the sight of the Lord. Time after time in the book of Judges the writer explained how the Israelites would become unfaithful to God and begin to worship their idols. In return God would subject them to terrorism from their enemies. In Judges 6, the Lord turned the Israelites over into the hands of the Midianites of the land of Midian. The Midianites were a mischievous clan who teamed up with the Amalekites and other eastern clans to terrorize the Israelites.

Together, they would hide in caves, tents, and dens in the mountains to attack the agriculture and livestock of Israel. Every time Israel stock and produce would increase, the Midianites, Amalekites, and eastern clans would come and destroy it. Because the land of Israel thrived off its agricultural advantages, destroying the agriculture of Israel was devastating to Israel's economy. This was terrorism to the Israelites, but God allowed it because the Israelites had turned away from God and forgotten all the wonderful things God had done for them. This devastation made Israel cry out for God's help. God answered their prayer by choosing a weak man to show His power. Judges 6,

> The angel of the Lord came and sat down under the oak in Ophrah that belonged to Joash the Abiezrite, where his son Gideon was threshing wheat in a winepress to keep it from the Midianites. When the angel of the Lord appeared to Gideon, he said, "The Lord is with you, mighty warrior."

"Pardon me, my lord," Gideon replied, "but if the Lord is with us, why has all this happened to us? Where are all his wonders that our ancestors told us about when they said, 'Did not the Lord bring us up out of Egypt?' But now the Lord has abandoned us and given us into the hand of Midian."

The Lord turned to him and said, "Go in the strength you have and save Israel out of Midian's hand. Am I not sending you?"

"Pardon me, my lord," Gideon replied, "but how can I save Israel? My clan is the weakest in Manasseh, and I am the least in my family."

The Lord answered, "I will be with you, and you will strike down all the Midianites, leaving none alive." (Judges 6:11–16 NIV)

Addressing Weakness

Here we see God calling a man in despair named Gideon to be raised to be a deliverer against the Midianites. Gideon was just a poor son of a farmer, Joash. What does He know about defeating enemies? Gideon was hiding grain in a winepress where it does not belong to disguise the grain so that the Midianites would not destroy the little grain that his family had left.

The grain in the winepress was an example of how God would use a man of agriculture to defeat the terrorist. Gideon was like the grain in the winepress. Gideon was a farmer not a fighter. Gideon would be considered as out of place in a battle as wheat in a winepress. Gideon's specialty was horticulture, not warfare. Gideon understood his weakness and openly expressed his weakness after the Lord called Him to defeat the Midianites. Let's look again at verses 14 and 15: "The Lord turned to him and said, "Go in the strength you have and save Israel out of Midian's hand. Am I not sending you?" "Pardon me, my lord," Gideon replied, "but how can I save Israel? My clan is the weakest in Manasseh, and I am the least in my family."

Gideon openly expressed his weakness to God. He was of the weakest tribe called Manasseh. He was the weakest man out of all the tribe. Gideon lived his life the way he saw himself. He thought he was not capable of defeating his terrorist. He was terrified and weak. His expressed weakness was his lifestyle. Gideon saw his life one way, but God designed another life for Gideon. Gideon saw himself as a weak farmer; God saw a fierce warrior.

God listened to Gideon's expressed weakness and addressed it. Gideon told the angel of the Lord who he thought he was, the angel of the Lord told Gideon who he really was. In verse 15 Gideon expressed his weakness about image. In verse 16 God addressed Gideon's weakness with His identity. Verse 16 says, "The Lord answered, 'I will be with you, and you will strike down all the Midianites, leaving nonalive.'" God addressed Gideon's weakness by giving him His assurance. Gideon was insecure about his purpose; God secured him with His presence.

I encourage you to read the rest of the book of Judges, in particular Judges 6. You will learn that Gideon was insecure about what God had told him about His calling and he asked for several supernatural signs. God responded to his request and showed Gideon the signs that he requested. God's command to Gideon was that he had to tear down all the idols that his father had built and build an altar to the Lord in their place. Gideon rose that morning and tore down all the idols of Baal that His father had built. From then on, the Spirit of the Lord resided with Gideon and he began to do exploits.

There is a beautiful revelation in this part of the story of Gideon that God will alter us on the altar. When we allow God to tear down our idols (our habits, addictions, mindsets, relationships) and submit to God in those places, God will make the necessary adjustments to our lives for His glory. When we take the power from our idols and false gods, God himself will empower us to do what He has purposed us to do.

The altar is a broken place where we lay our lives down before God and submit to His will. The altar is a secret meeting place between us and God. The altar is a place of sacrifice. The altar is a place of presentation. We present ourselves, our weaknesses, our strengths, and offer them before God as a sacrifice to Him.

Apostle Paul writes this to the church in Rome in Romans 12:

> Therefore, I urge you, brothers and sisters, in view of God's mercy, to offer your bodies as a living sacrifice, holy and pleasing to God—this is your true and proper worship. Do not conform to the pattern of this world, but be transformed by the renewing of your mind. Then you will be able to test and approve what God's will is—his good, pleasing and perfect will. (Romans 12:1–2 NIV)

It is God's will that He breaks your lifestyle of weakness on the altar, so that He can alter your life to do His perfect will. We are not to be conformed to the world but are to be transformed by the renewing of our minds in

Christ Jesus. God wants to change our self-view from how the world sees us, to how He sees us. We must present ourselves before God, tear down our idols, and allow God to alter us on the altar or the secret place with Him.

Gideon went on to fight against the Midianites as the Spirit of God was upon Him. He and his gathered troops destroyed the Midianites and all their allies. God used a terrified man to destroy his people's terrorists. God turned Gideon's welfare mentality into a warfare mentality. Gideon went from hiding grain from his enemies in a winepress to boldly destroying the enemies he once hid from. God used Gideon and 300 men to defeat thousands of Midianites. The story is in Judges chapter 7. God used Gideon and transformed the terror in his soul into His territory. Remember this, God will always raise a Gideon to defeat Midian. . No matter what your terror is, God is raising a warrior in you who will defeat what has terrorized you and your family for years. God will change your terror into your territory, but first you must allow your weakness to be addressed by God. Let God deal with the weak areas.

Embrace the strengthening process. Embrace the initial shock. Let God raise the standard in your life. If you endure this process, God will make your addressed place of weakness into an entry for His glory and power to be displayed. Your weakness will become God's entry way to display his power. God allowed the weakness so that He could bring glory through your weak place, and your weakness is being used by God to show you and others just how powerful God is.

The strength that you will carry is not your own strength, but the strength of the Lord. Apostle Paul writes in 2 Corinthians 12:

> Even if I should choose to boast, I would not be a fool, because I would be speaking the truth. But I refrain, so no one will think more of me than is warranted by what I do or say, or because of these surpassingly great revelations. Therefore, to keep me from becoming conceited, I was given a thorn in my flesh, a messenger of Satan, to torment me. Three times I pleaded with the Lord to take it away from me. But he said to me, "My grace is sufficient for you, for my power is made perfect in weakness." Therefore I will boast all the more gladly about my weaknesses, so that Christ's power may rest on me. That is why, for Christ's sake, I delight in weaknesses, in insults, in hardships, in persecutions, in difficulties. For when I am weak, then I am strong. (2 Corinthians 12:6–10 NIV)

Apostle Paul is simply explaining that God uses our weakness to show us Christ's power in us and through us.

The Lord allows us to have weak areas to remind us that it's His great power working through us and not our own. That's why God calls us to do things that we feel like we are not strong enough to do. He shows us and others His great power in our weakness. His grace and power prevail in our weakness. His power to deliver, save, heal, and forgive are all displayed in our weaknesses. Our weaknesses are His entry way.

Present your weaknesses to God. God will address the reasons you have them and He will bring His strength through your weaknesses empowering you to touch the world. God is going to change your story of weakness into a testimony of His greatness. Your weaknesses belong to God. No one should ever be able to identify you through your weakness. The only one who should be able to see your weaknesses is God. Stop exposing your own weaknesses to people. People cannot help you with the strength you need to overcome your weakness without God sending them. People can give you general advice, but they can't give you specific instruction without God. People cannot handle your weaknesses. The place where His strength meets your weakness will be used by God as a meeting ground between you and Him where you'll give Him your weakness, and He will give you His strength. People only see the situation of your weakness; God sees the sanctuary of your weakness. God wants to dwell in our weakness. When we present our weakness to Him, so He can dwell there, His ability will extend where our ability ends. God reaches beyond our dilemma. God allows our weaknesses to humble us to and house Himself in us.

There's a difference between flaws and weaknesses. A flaw is a mark, fault, or other imperfection that mars a substance or object. A weakness is the state or condition of lacking strength. Flaws are unique marks that cause imperfections. Weakness is a condition that creates limitations. Don't confuse flaws with weaknesses. We are not perfect. We all have flaws. We all have things in our lives that show imperfection. Some may have big noses, some may be short, some may have speech problems, some may have vision problems, some may have troubles reading and some may have troubles hearing. All these flaws show imperfection, but they still make us unique from others. Flaws are noticeable, weaknesses are hidden until revealed. Sometimes we allow our flaws to become weaknesses instead of allowing God to work out our flaws. Some flaws can't be erased and need to be embraced. God wants us to embrace our imperfections because our imperfections show His perfection. God doesn't want us to embrace our weaknesses, God wants to embrace our weaknesses and work through our weakness. God's strength will erase our weaknesses.

III

Private Development

Desperation is the appetite of desire. When you think about how different cultures came to be across the world, you will see a group of people who invented and innovated while living with a set of daily struggles. Culture is born out of struggle. Edible delicacies and recipes around the world were created out of limited food supply. Basically, they cooked what they had, and started being creative with it. This method has created some of the most deliciously cherished dishes to date. Creative struggle has a way of transforming scraps into gourmet meals.

Language, traditions, and fashion were born out of the struggle of a group of people who used the scraps to produce something never seen before. This is what happened to the Israelites in the wilderness. God taught them their culture in the middle of the wilderness. The Israelites became accustomed to Egyptian culture. I want to briefly explain Genesis 37 to Exodus 13 in scripture, you will see God bringing the Israelite family to Egypt through Jacob's son Joseph. The Israelite family multiplied in the land of Egypt and were enslaved by the Egyptians because the pharaoh was afraid that the Israelites were growing too massive and taking over Egypt.

The Israelites were in Egypt for 430 years before God delivered them out of the land. In those 430 years, the Israelites adopted the culture of Egypt. If God did not allow them to go into slavery, there would have been no Israelite culture, just Egypt. God brought the Israelites out of Egypt and through the wilderness so that He could break them away from Egyptian culture and teach them the culture that He expected them to have. God gave them their culture in the wilderness so they could know how to behave in the land He promised them. This process took forty years. All the language, fashion, food, and traditions of the land of Israel were born in the wilderness.

God uses desperation to fuel the hunger of expectation. Desperation is the creative space that God uses to raise the hunger for exploration to find resources. The 400 in 1 Samuel 22 were desperate for a change. They were deprived and despaired and so was David. God mixed the two desperate positions to produce a strong tribe and a strong leader. All the fighting tactics, weapon strategies, bodybuilding, diet plans, and wisdom of David and the 400 were born in the cave. This cave was a place of desperation. Desperation was the training ground for the outcome desired. Desperation uses discomfort to agitate the comfortability of lack. Desperation grabs the soul's attention and speaks to the soul that something needs to change. Desperation is a demand for action.

Discomfort is the initiation of development. When a person is body building, they violently disrupt their muscles when they lift weight or do certain workouts. Muscles must be ripped during a workout for muscle growth and strengthening. This is a discomforting event for the body. Pushing through the discomfort is the method for achieving the desired results. When we deprive ourselves of comfort and embrace discomfort in our desperation, we will see new development arrive in our lives. We will learn new things and go to new places with the assurance of the development that has taken place.

The Importance of the Cave

The cave of Adullam was an important training ground for David and the 400 because it was a private place of development where David had the chance to train and develop the 400 without interruption. David was able to target the individuals' personal weaknesses as well as the collective weakness of the 400. In the cave David was able to use disruption without interruption and to use inside criticism without outside criticisms interfering with the training process. If David would have trained the 400 amongst King Saul's troops, the development of the 400 would have been poisoned by King Saul's influence.

The king either would have requested to kill the 400 or he would have requested to recruit the 400. Either way, David would not be able to teach the 400 the fear of the Lord but rather the fear of King Saul. David's loyalty to King Saul would have spoken louder than David's obedience to God.

God used the cave of Adullam to transform David from an entertainer into a trainer. Everything David did before the cave was in service to King Saul. David's life was centered on entertaining Saul. Whether he was coaching King Saul's troops or playing music for King Saul, David did everything in service to Saul. God transformed David from being in service to his earthly king, to being in service to His Heavenly King. God converted David from pursuing the training of King Saul's army to pursuing the training of the Lord's army.

God used the private place to convert David from a weak man among weaklings into a commander and his strong army. Adullam was a private place of conversion. Conversion is the process of changing from one form to another. God used David to develop the 400 in this secret place. God used this secrecy for David and his clan's conversion. In this secret place there were no interruptions, no distraction, just development.

In Hebrew *Adullam* means "hiding place." According to *A Hebrew and English Lexicon of the Old Testament*, the Arabic word *adula* means "turn aside." This implies that Adullam means "refuge." There is a beautiful revelation in this. David was hiding in a place of refuge, and the 400 who came there to join him were refugees. The revelation is that God hid David in the place of refuge so that the 400 could come to a place of refuge. God used David to train the 400 not just to seek refuge but to be refuge. They were looking for refuge but not looking in the mirror to see refuge. God used David's hiding place as a training place for the 400 hundred to become God's refuge against King Saul.

In our lives, God is using secret places to develop us into what He is calling us to be. Some of these places are unlikely training places. Some of us are hidden at a job, in a family, in a career, in a relationship, and some are even hidden in terrible situations. We are uncomfortable and miserable, but God is using our discomfort to develop something in us that we did not know was there. Without these hiding places, we would never reach the potential of what God wants us to be.

Sometimes we think that our hidden places are a refuge where we run to hide but really our hiding place is where God chooses to hide us. A secret place with God is not a serene place where there are no problems or worries. A true secret place with God is wherever God chooses to hide us, even if it is a place of chaos. True secrecy with God is a place of choosing to rest in Him in the place where He chooses to hide us. David took refuge in a cave in the middle of running from his enemies. David didn't find the secret place; God provided the secret place.

We must ask God to provide the secret place for us to be transformed and we must stop looking for a secret place for ourselves. Some of us think we have found our secret place, but really we have just found temporary relief. We find false secret places in sex, drugs, money, relationships, habits, pornography, alcohol, and partying. These false secret places only weaken our resistance to fight against the enemy of our souls. The true secret place of God builds our resistance against the enemy. We must ask God to provide privacy for us. When God provides the secret place, He will empower us. The false secret places we find for ourselves are places of devourment, but the true secret places are places of empowerment.

The secret place is a resting place but not a relaxing place. The private place with God is a meeting place with God. God uses privacy to work on us, to prepare us to become what He is calling us to be. We are drawn into the secret place looking for answers, but we emerge from the secret place being the answer. Don't count it strange when God calls you into a private place. When God calls you to sit on the side lines, it's to improve you. Being in a private place with God means that we aren't going to be as active as we once were. Some of us were active but not productive. When God sits you down, He plans to set you up. Be still and know that He is God. Don't force yourself into activity. Let God work on you. You are not out of commission but under construction.

God's construction of your life looks like destruction, but the intention is different. God is using the tearing down to employ you, not to destroy you. Your secret place in the Lord is just like a construction site. The Lord has roped off your construction site so that construction can take place without interruption. God is using this private place to construct a masterpiece out of your misery. These are the four ways God uses privacy:

1.) God uses privacy to transform poverty into property.

Poverty is another word for hardship. God uses hardship to teach a harsh lesson about possession. Hardship is an opportunity to possess. Hardship triggers a need for more. God uses hardship to make slaves hunger for their own. It is a call for freedom. Hardship turns renters into owners. It sparks the hunger for the quest to possess. Without hardship we would be complacent in a position and place where God did not intend for us to have or be. Recall the Israelites who were comfortable in Egypt. They were complacent until they were hit with hardship. They would have never quested to the promised land without the hardship God allowed. God used their struggle to transform hardship into ownership.

2.) God uses privacy to transform irritation into irrigation.

Irrigation is the supply of water to land or crops to help growth, typically by means of channels dug into the earth. The main thing that sticks out to me about this definition are the words *supply, growth,* and *channel.* Irritation is the state of feeling annoyed, impatient, or slightly angry. Spiritually, irritation is a channel of God disrupting our natural state to bring a supply of growth to a place that would die without supply. Irritation is an attention grabber that causes us to reevaluate our growth. Irritation will bring out the worst in you but also instill you with the best of you. The process of irrigation may disturb the natural state of the land because of the digging of the channels to supply water, but it brings growth to places in dire need of growth. God uses irritation as a canal to disturb your natural state to bring supernatural growth in a place of urgent need.

3.) God uses privacy to transform agitation into ability.

Agitation is a state of anxiety or nervous excitement. Anxiety is a longing to know the outcome. God uses the spirit of fear and anxiety to create ability. God already knows the outcome, He allows us to be agitated so that we can switch positions from longing to know the outcome, to longing to show the outcome. Agitation is a creative space where God enables us to develop unknown abilities. Agitation wakes up hidden abilities that need to be strengthened. God uses agitation to help us long to be what we don't see.

The apostle Paul writes to the church of Philippi about anxiousness in Philippians 4, where he says, "Be anxious for nothing, but in everything by prayer and supplication, with thanksgiving, let your requests be made known to God; and the peace of God, which surpasses all understanding, will guard your hearts and minds through Christ Jesus" (Phil. 4:6–7 NKJV). The word does not state "Feel anxious for nothing," it says "Be anxious for nothing." Paul never stated that we will never feel anxious but instructs us not to be anxious. Paul proves that our anxiousness produces ability by telling us that anxiousness is an opportunity to request guidance from God. It's okay to approach God feeling anxious but we should never approach God being anxious. Approach God to request, not to suggest. Approach Him with produced ability and not with produced anxiousness. Paul makes this point again in 2 Timothy chapter 1: " For God has not given us a spirit of fear, but of power and of love and of a sound mind" (2 Tim. 1:7 NKJV).

4.) God uses privacy to transform emotion into information.

God has given us emotions to heighten experiences so that we can grasp lessons, knowledge, and concepts. Emotions are to be used as indicators, not dictators.

Emotions should never be in control. The Holy Spirit uses our emotions to indicate what is on the mind of God. When your emotions are allowed to lead you, they will cause you to be lost in an emotional state. Emotions are supposed to point to information. God uses sadness, anger, happiness, and our other emotions to make people seek for information and answers. God uses privacy to work on our emotions so that we can properly use our emotions, so that our emotions won't use us. Our emotions should never lead us. We are to lead our emotions to the Holy Spirit, and He will use our emotions to bring us information that holds answers. Proverbs 28:2 states "He who trusts in his own heart is a fool, but he who walks wisely will be delivered." God wants us to yield our emotions to wisdom, wisdom will release the answers.

The cave of Adullam was a secluded place that was initially for the purpose of refuge. God used the cave for the purpose of reconstruction. The seclusion of David and the 400 was vital. The cave was transformed from a place of pity into a place of preparation. It transformed from a hiding place into a campground where David had the chance to exclusively train the 400, changing them from refugees into a regiment. It was important that David kept the training place private.

There is no scriptural record about how David trained the troops. As we read further into 1 Samuel chapter 22, we see David and the 400 started to venture out on military exploits. The beginning of the chapter stated the origin of David and the 400, but the chapter never explained the preparation of the 400. God knew that David and the 400 would be in a very vulnerable condition while training. David and the 400 were already broken, discouraged, and weakened. The cave was a remote place that God would use to declutter the hearts of David and the 400. David was responsible for dealing with the fragile fearful hearts of the 400 and strengthening them into firm, fearless hearts. David would have to apply pressure to the 400 to raise their standards and ability. Privacy is the best place to challenge weakness and strengthen flaws into strengths. Nobody was allowed to see this process except God, David, and the 400.

This is the perfect time to say, what happened in the cave, stayed in the cave. This phrase derives from the famous Las Vegas slogan "what happens in Vegas, stays in Vegas." Also, many families use the motto "what happens in this house, stays in this house." Although that mindset in a home can be harmful, in this case the phrase is appropriate, especially when God is carrying you through a transformation.

You must remain private like the 400, don't expose yourself during training. Don't come out of the cave until the process is done. You don't have to go around explaining the process you are going through to others. You don't have to try to convince others that you are in a transformation process. If you come out of the cave too early, it could be damaging to your process.

If David would have exposed the 400 too early or even told others where he was training them, King Saul would have had the opportunity of locating them and ending what David was called to do with the 400. King Saul would've had the option to kill David and the 400 or to recruit the 400 for himself. It was important that David and the 400 could not be located. Even the Philistines would have taken the troops captive and stolen their war tactics. It's quite silly to include the metaphor about pirates in this paragraph but it relates to this wisdom in so many ways. The noun form of the word *pirate* means "a person who attacks and robs ships at sea." The verb *pirate* means "to use or reproduce (another's work) for profit without permission, usually in contravention of patent or copyright." Pirates steal treasures and valuables for personal gain without the permission of the rightful owner. We must stay clear of piracy by not being located while in privacy. It was important that David and the 400 could not be located. I want to give the same wisdom to you in this process, don't be located. Remain private. Hide and heal. Train and transform. Quietness is important in this season. The only person who should be able to see your weakness is God, your trainer, and the wise counsel that God has provided you with. Premature exposure can cause permanent damage. Avoid exposing your process of growth.

The military takes their recruits to a remote place for boot camp so that they can intensively deal with the characters of the recruits. Their goal is to turn regular civilians into strong military personnel. Bringing the recruits to a remote place is a strategic method so that the training process is uninterrupted and so that they can challenge the new cadets to convert their mindset to the standards of the armed forces. The trainers of the armed forces have utilized the wisdom that privacy is best for development

A baby growing in the womb must stay secluded in the womb. If the doctor decided to induce labor and birth the baby out of its mother in the first or second trimester, it would cause major pregnancy complications. At the beginning of the pregnancy, the baby cannot survive outside of the seclusion of its mother's womb. If exposed prematurely to the world, the baby could face severe health complications. Both baby and mother could die if the process of birth is damaged. The baby will be at its healthiest state when the pregnancy is full term.

During this process of conversion, stay secluded. Go full term. Stay in the secret place with God. Stop calling on others to explain your process. They are outsiders looking in, and they do not understand the cave that you are in. Their advice, conversation, and even discouragement can damage you in this process. Let the process take place without explanation. If exposed to the outside world too early, you will stunt your growth and hold up the process of transformation. Don't reach outside of the cave, stay committed to the cave and to the process of transformation. Stay committed to the secret place. Don't tell others the secrets you learn about God, your leader, and yourself in the secret place. God doesn't want you to tell the secrets; He wants you to become the secrets. As hard as it is, let God isolate you. There is a difference between you isolating yourself and God isolating you. When you isolate yourself, you are attempting to hide from your problems. When God isolates you, He is putting you into a secluded private place to transform you into the answers to the problems you face. Stay committed to secrecy with God. God only tells secrets to those who will stay committed to the secret place. Allow secrecy to become your scenery.

IV

THE DISCIPLINE OF EMBARRASSMENT

The definition of defeat is to win a victory over someone in a battle or other contest, to overcome or beat an opponent. Defeat can be looked at from two angles. On one hand, defeat can be looked at as a good thing, a victorious event where a person has overcome someone or something they were battling against. In this case a person is defeating someone else. On the other hand, a person can be defeated by a person or something that they are battling. In this case a person is accepting defeat. Either viewpoint is called defeat. Defeat can either be a moment of domination or a moment of devastation. One can defeat or be defeated. To defeat someone is an action; to be defeated is a reaction. Defeating an opponent brings on a mentality of confidence and satisfaction. When a person is defeated, they have two choices about the mentality that they are going to have. The defeated person can look at their defeat as oppression or they can look at their defeat as an opportunity.

When a person looks at their defeat as an oppression, they can only see things through the eyes of the oppressed. The person who looks through the eyes of oppression lives their life with the mindset that there is no advantage. The oppressed person feels as if there are no options left, so they do not look for options. They are behaving just like a doctor who feels they have run out of options to save the life of their patient and decides to inform the family and to make the patient comfortable to die. Oppression sedates the defeated so that they can lay down and die a slow death. Oppression makes you comfortable in your defeat. The person who looks at defeat through the eyes of oppression doesn't look for any chances to receive redemption, they only look for opportunities to die or escape. Either they look for ways to become comfortable in their oppression or they look for ways to run away from the place that is oppressing them. Looking at defeat through the eyes of oppression paralyzes your ability to learn how to overcome what you have been defeated by.

Those who look at defeat through the eyes of opportunity look for ways to overthrow their oppressor, even if it costs them their lives. Looking through the eyes of opportunity we see defeat as a lesson. Those who see defeat through the eye of opportunity watch and study every point of their defeat and their oppressor to learn ways to defeat them. A person looking at defeat through the eyes of opportunity studies where they went wrong and what they can do better. Those who look for opportunity in defeat are preparing themselves for their next chance to win. The eyes of oppression are closed, the eyes of opportunity are on constant watch. Although, we walk by faith and not sight as believers (2 Cor. 5:7), faith is the lens that the eyes of opportunity look through. They see the opportunity for victory in defeat. It's an opportunity for recalculation.

Those who look for opportunity in defeat have learned to embrace embarrassment. Embarrassment is a feeling of self-consciousness, shame, or awkwardness. Embarrassment is the worst feeling ever and it can be very degrading. But those who have embraced embarrassment don't allow the degrading feeling to downgrade them, they use it to upgrade them. There is a sweet substance of discipline inside the bitter taste of embarrassment. Embracing embarrassment teaches us how to stay on our toes and in the position of a student. Embarrassment is to be studied. Embarrassment is to be evaluated. In this private place of training, embrace the embarrassment of your defeat.

Training challenges you to evaluate the embarrassment of what is defeating you and embrace the opportunity for growth that it brings. Embracing embarrassment brings discipline; defeat brings opportunity. In this private place of training, embarrassment will be used as a tool to advance you. Regret is not supposed to terrorize you but prioritize you. God is turning your regret into respect.

God is discarding your regret of your defeat and raising your respect for the opportunity to learn from defeat. He is turning your humiliation into humility. God is tearing down your pride against the lesson that you need to learn and humbling you to follow His principles.

In 1 Samuel 22:2 the discontented, indebted, and distressed group of people came to David oppressed by their defeat. They had defeated mindsets; it was up to David to teach them that there is opportunity to learn to overthrow their oppressors in their defeat. David had to train them not to live in embarrassment but to learn from embarrassment. David shifted their mentalities to change their embarrassments into enhancements.

God uses places of embarrassment to humble the wicked places of pride in us. These wicked places of pride were built around our lives to shield the weak areas in our lives from being exposed. We don't want our weak areas exposed out of fear that we will be wounded more in the places where we are weak. Pride is a defensive mechanism that we use to cover up weakness. The definition of pride is a feeling of deep pleasure or satisfaction derived from one's own achievements, from the achievements of those with whom one is closely associated, or from qualities or possessions that are widely admired. We build up a fake sense of pride that ultimately hurts us more.

Pride does more damage than good. Pride is a dead end. Pride makes us feel like we are "know it alls" who are too good to humble ourselves and learn. Pride can be misinterpreted as strength. Pride give weakness a voice. Pride plus weakness equals wickedness. Wickedness is simply longing to do the opposite of what God wants and desires. Wickedness goes against the authority of God. When we allow pride to settle in a place of weakness, it will create a place of rebellion against God. Wickedness is where weaknesses run wild. We close our ears to God in places of pride and pride builds our rebellion against God, which is known as wickedness.

We know from Scripture that God detests the proud and the haughty. Proverbs 16:5 (NIV) says, "The Lord detests all the proud of heart. Be sure of this: They will not go unpunished." Proverbs 16:18 "Pride goes before destruction, a haughty spirit before a fall." Proverbs 11:2 "When pride comes, then comes disgrace, but with humility comes wisdom." Pride pushes us away from God; humility draws us to God. Pride's motive is to impress others and to boost the self. Humility's motive is to serve others and to live beyond self. God uses embarrassment to transform our places of pride to places of healing.

Embarrassment is a place of exposure. God exposes our pride through embarrassment and destroys its motive so that the Spirit of God can reside where pride once was. Humility brings us into the position of submission to God. It helps us to follow the Spirit and not our heart of flesh. The flesh is prideful and when we submit to our flesh, we submit to rebellion against God. The flesh is carnal and it wants to do the opposite of what the Spirit of God requires. Those who live according to the flesh have their minds set on what the flesh desires; but those who live in accordance with the Spirit have their minds set on what the Spirit desires.

Apostle Paul speaks to this in Romans 8:

> The mind governed by the flesh is death, but the mind governed by the Spirit is life and peace. The mind governed by the flesh is hostile to God; it does not submit to God's law, nor can it do so. Those who are in the realm of the flesh cannot please God. You, however, are not in the realm of the flesh but are in the realm of the Spirit, if indeed the Spirit of God lives in you. And if anyone does not have the Spirit of Christ, they do not belong to Christ. (Romans 8:6–9 NIV)

The flesh operates in pride. God uses embarrassment or humiliation to overcome pride and bring humility. Humility is a place where God's Spirit flows. Embarrassment causes prideful people to defend themselves with pride, and pride uses their place of weakness for wickedness. Embarrassment causes humbled people to submit to God, and God uses their weakness as an entry to show His great power. Through Christ, our weaknesses become areas of communion with God. God draws out affections from our afflictions. Without our weak areas, some of us would not even care about fellowship with God.

God uses humiliation to break us down, so our rebellion can turn into repentance. God wants us to build an altar in the place of our pride. We build idols in our idle places. Our idle places are on reserve for God to use. But we build places of pride in our hearts so that we can have pseudo answers to unanswered places in us. The unanswered place belongs to God, He wants to answer those places at a specific time for His glory. Out of pride we have built idols in ordained places.

God has allowed places in us to be weak so that we can commune with Him in His power in those places. As a substitute we build idols in those places. We build places of rebellion against God in places where communion with God should be. God uses embarrassment to shake down our idols, and He can use those weak spots in our lives to move in a supernatural way.

Let God Break the Heart

God is a heartbreaker. God will break your heart to put the heart back together in the way that He intended it to be. God breaks the heart in order to transform it. God will break the heart, but He will not leave the heartbroken. God breaks the heart so that He can write His intentions and goals on the heart, in order that the heart can function in reverence of God and not in reverence of rebellion. God breaks the heart to create it anew. Transformation cannot take place until the heart has been restored or replaced.

Restoration of the heart is a process through which God carries the heart that has been damaged from situations and misfortune. A heart that needs restoration is still a good heart, it just needs to be healed. These are the hearts that have dealt with betrayal, misfortune, regret, and humiliation. These hearts look through the eye of expressed weakness and mistrust. These hearts have grown sick with disappointment and are becoming wicked due to hurt and constant disloyalty. God must break the weak, sickened heart, clean it, and put it back together again. God must cleanse the heart that needs restoration, so that the heart can function without motives and agenda. God wants our hearts to be well. When our hearts are well, we will carry out His perfect will without agenda.

Sometimes when I watch superhero shows and movies, I start to feel bad for the villain when it's time for the villain to face punishment. Usually, somewhere in the movie or show, you will find out why the villain became evil. Some of the villains were raised evil or were evil from the beginning (I will come back to this one), but some villains become evil because of the amount of trauma, rejection, and betrayal they'd faced in their youth. The villain finally decides to fight back. Instead of learning how to stand up for themselves, they learn how to use evil to bring vengeance to those who've hurt them. This eventually pushes them to embrace a criminal mindset. These villains began to have evil motives and try to carry them out because their hearts are sick and bitter.

The sick heart never intends to have an evil agenda at first, but evil agendas eventually grow, causing the heart to embrace deceit and evil. Deceit organically forms in the heart because of the curse of sin. God searches the heart, breaks it, and then cleanses it so that it can be well and in reverence of Him. Jeremiah 17 says, "The heart is deceitful above all things, and desperately wicked: who can know it? I the Lord search the heart, I try the reins, even to give every man according to his ways, and according to the fruit of his doings" (Jer. 17:9–10 KJV). The heart that is sick is desperate for wickedness, but a healed heart is desperate for righteousness in God.

Let God Create the Heart

The replacement of a heart is a process that God uses to take away a heart that has been destroyed, one that has been raised in evil and taught evil from the beginning and replaces it with a brand-new clean heart. The heart that needs to be replaced was bred in wickedness and was never taught to do well or seek for righteous things. The destroyed heart is beyond sick, it is diseased or even dead. This is a heart that longs to do evil and seeks for opportunities to be selfish or rebel against God. The destroyed heart is not broken but shattered. The destroyed heart cannot be restored but must be replaced.

Certain criminal minded people were taught from young ages how to embrace criminal activity as a lifestyle. Most criminals watched their parents and loved ones commit crimes, do drugs, and go through cycles of being in and out of jail. Some of these people were taught through demonstration or even words how to commit crimes and have embraced criminal activity as a lifestyle.

I remember watching a documentary about an LA gang member. He stated that he was born into a gang—his whole family was in a gang—and that he had no choice but to gang bang because it was his household's lifestyle. Street life was the way of life for his family. He felt that there was no other way. His heart knew nothing else but gang banging and all he wanted to do was to live and die in the streets.

The destroyed heart sees no way out. They try to do good but always resort back to evil because evil is instinctive for them. The damaged heart doesn't function properly, but the destroyed heart does not function at all. The destroyed heart is calloused and dead to the love of God. The chest is not a resting place for a destroyed heart but a grave. God must replace the whole heart, to give the person new goals, intentions, instincts, and purpose. The destroyed heart is desperate for wickedness, but the replaced heart is desperate for the things of God. David says this in Psalm 119: "Their hearts are callous and unfeeling, / but I delight in your law. / It was good for me to be afflicted / so that I might learn your decrees" (Ps. 119:70–71 NIV).

Open heart surgery is a surgery where the chest is opened, and an operation takes place on the different parts of the heart like arteries, valves, and tissues. Although it is a painful process, it is a private process. The operating room is a private undisturbed place. The doctors must pay close attention to the heart to save a heart and save a life.

What we look at as opposition to the heart is really the operation of the heart. Allowing God to perform surgery on our heart is a painful process. The heart is not being ruined but repaired. God must open the heart to operate on it. God is exposing the things that are wrong with our hearts so that He can repair the damage and replace the destroyed heart. God is opening you to operate on you. Your heart is not broken; your heart is open.

In the process of God operating on the heart, He also programs the heart with His desires. God cleanses the heart of all the wicked things that were written on it and writes His laws on the heart. When God writes His laws on our hearts, our reverence for His will heightens. When the Lord writes His laws on our hearts, He redirects our desire from our own desires to the ones He has designed for us to have. Through Christ Jesus, the Son of God, the laws of God have been written on the tablet of our hearts so we will not depart from God's desires. After our heart has been cleansed and filled with God's Word, we will long to live out God's desires, and never depart from His will. God transforms the departing of our hearts from His law into an imparting of His law into our hearts.

Four Key Scriptures of God's Operation of the Heart:

1.) Deuteronomy 8:2 (NLT) says, "Remember how the Lord your God led you through the wilderness for these forty years, humbling you and testing you to prove your character, and to find out whether or not you would obey his commands."

2.) Jeremiah 31:33 (NIV) says, "This is the covenant I will make with the people of Israel after that time," declares the Lord. "I will put my law in their minds and write it on their hearts. I will be their God, and they will be my people.

3.) Proverbs 3:5–6 (NIV) says "Trust in the Lord with all your hear and lean not on your own understanding; in all your ways submit to him, and he will make your paths straight."

4.) Psalm 27:14 (KJV) says, "Wait on the Lord: be of good courage, and he shall strengthen thine heart: wait, I say, on the Lord."

Enclosed Exposure

The clan of 400 who joined David were trained in an enclosed place. In this place we will assume that David used methods of embarrassment to break down the clan's disposition of weakness to bring them to a disposition of warriors. The embarrassment that we are talking about in this chapter is not a point-and-laugh type of embarrassment. We are talking about the topic of exposure. David exposed the clan's weakness to God as well as to them so that God could use David to address their weakness and strengthen it. In the private place of training, David had to expose the unaddressed weak places to make way for God's strength to flow through.

The word *exposure* means "the state of being exposed to contact with something." When God embarrasses the wickedness of the heart, He exposes the heart's motives. Exposure is necessary for transformation because exposing the heart extricates the wicked desires of the heart that cause the person to believe that they are a slave to their weakness. The wicked heart has an evil agenda in our weakness. God uses embarrassment to expose the agenda of the heart for purposes of recreation.

A married man or woman who has an affair with someone outside of their marriage is usually fueled by the lust of not getting caught. To be hidden in something forbidden gives the flesh an astronomical arousal. The flesh is extremely aroused by whatever displeases God.

People who sneak and sleep around on their spouses usually love the arousal of the secret that they are hiding. The flesh always craves the forbidden fruit. Whatever God says don't do, that's what the flesh wants to do the most. Once the affair is exposed, the arousal leaves because the wickedness is not hidden anymore.

God is not exposing you to the public places but to the private places. In training transformation God exposes our private parts. Yes, you read it right. God exposes our private parts in private places. I am not talking about the private part of our physical bodies, I'm talking about the private parts of our heart that we won't let God into. These are the parts of us that we choose to hide from God. Just like Adam and Eve in Genesis 3 who hid themselves from God because they disobeyed Him and realized that they were naked, their private parts were exposed. Noticed in that story, that they were naked before God when God cursed them and put them out of the garden. Before God put them out of the garden, He covered their exposed parts with animal skin. Even though Adam and Eve were exposed before God in the private garden, God clothed their nakedness before He sent them out of the garden.

God is not going to expose the private parts of our hearts to the public. God will always cover us from the public. The public will always try to point out our nakedness. God will always clothe the ones that He's exposed. You are not exposed in public but exposed in private. No one can see the nakedness of your heart but God. God is using this exposure to take you from hiding your nakedness, to being covered in your nakedness by Him. God wants us to shift our perspective from hiding the private parts of our hearts from God to hiding the private parts of our hearts in God. God will clothe the exposed. The private parts are to be dealt with in private places.

Mark 14:51(NIV) reads, "A young man, wearing nothing but a linen garment, was following Jesus. When they seized him," A young man with a towel or a linen cloth was following Jesus as He was arrested. If you take the time to study this text more deeply, you will see that it has several interpretations about who the young man was and why he was in the garden with Christ at the time of His arrest. One interpretation is that Mark is the writer of this book. Some claim that the young man is about a young Mark and his introduction to Christ. Another interpretation is one that really stuck out to me, which is that it was a dead man from a nearby grave that was resurrected when Christ said "I am he" at the time of his arrest (John 4:26–27). When Jesus said "I am He" it made the guards, the chief priest, and teachers of the law fall to the ground. What awesome power Jesus has!

Studies show that the garment that the man was wearing was called a sindon. A sindon was used as a burial garment to cover the body of the person that died. The interpretation says that the power of Jesus's declaration "I am He" released resurrection power into the local cemetery. The interpretation states that the young man was once a dead man who was resurrected by the power of Christ and led to the place of Christ's arrest.

I want to digress for just a moment. God knows how to turn cemeteries into sanctuaries. Cemeteries house the dead. Sanctuaries house the living. In this scripture, the resurrection power of Christ brings life to the cemetery and changes it from a place of burial to a place of beholding. Christ's power changes memorials into testimonials. I have a few questions for you, my friend: Are you a cemetery or a sanctuary? Are we presenting the memorial of dead things or presenting the testimonial of living things? Are you holding on to dead things (memories, grudges, doctrines, lifestyles, rituals) or are you allowing new life to flow in you through Christ? Are you housing the dead or the living?

Back to the story: I have leaned towards the second interpretation of Mark 14:51. There is a beautiful revelation in this interpretation that applies to the lesson of how God uses exposure to cover our private parts (places of vulnerability). The man was dressed in a sindon or a burial cloth before he came into contact with Christ. Christ allowed the guards to snatch the man's burial clothes causing him to run away naked. The beautiful revelation is that although the man ran away naked, his nakedness was a sign of passing from death into life. The guards snatched what the young man used to cover himself. The problem is that the man was using burial clothes, funeral garments to cover his private parts. Jesus allowed the garment to be snatched as a sign that the man was going from his funeral to freedom. When the guards snatched his garment that disqualified him from the grave and sent him running away in freedom. The sindon (sin) was snatched from the man when he encountered Christ. The garment being snatched was allowed by God to show that God uses exposure to liberate us from the things that we think are covering us but that are really meant to bury us. No matter the interpretation you choose to believe, the fact is that the man ran away naked, afraid, and embarrassed.

If you read on to verse 54 in Mark 14, you'll see that the story goes on and mentions nothing else about the young man. The story focused on Jesus and not the nakedness of the man. The writer instantly focused on the trial of Christ. I've wondered why the man wasn't talked about after that. What happened to this young man after he ran away naked? Where did he run to? What was he feeling? The answer to those questions is that it doesn't matter because Christ covered him. No one was focused on the man's exposure because Christ covered him. Although the man ran away embarrassed because he thought that his private parts were exposed, we see that it really worked for his good. The guards snatched the man's burial shroud and Christ covered him in resurrection.

The young man's embarrassment was used to free the man from his grave, the embarrassment snatched his graveyard clothes. His embarrassment was really an act of God to cover him in Christ. What the man thought was an exposing moment was really a clothing moment. The young man's private parts weren't discovered but covered

God is doing the same thing for you in this transformation. God is exposing your vulnerabilities so that He can cover them. God exposes them so that you can stop attempting to cover them yourself. God wants to clothe you in the strength of Christ. He wants your vulnerable places to become valuable places, but you will never see the value if God does not allow your cemetery clothes to be snatched. Some of us have embraced the shame of what we try to hide. We are willing to die in our shameful places. We stroud ourselves with spiritual burial garments and claim that we will be weak in these areas until we die. God must expose these private parts to let you see that He can shroud your shame in His glory and cover for you what you are trying to hide on your own.

Be naked and unashamed before your Creator. This is what he intended for Adam and Eve. This is what we now have in Christ. We are covered. God is covering you in His glory. I know you think that the public will see your private parts if your burial clothes are snatched, but God allows your garment to be snatched so that He can shroud you in strength and life. The public will not see your nakedness. They will only see His glory. Let God cover you.

Once God covers our nakedness, he issues armor to us so that we can stand as kingdom soldiers. The covering of God turns our nakedness into sacredness. Just like when he covered Adam and Eve in the garden of Eden. They appeared sacred before they appeared naked. They knew that they were sacred before they knew that they were naked. Deceit and sin banished our sacredness with God and exposed our nakedness to the earth. Christ has taken the shame of our nakedness; through Him we are now covered in sacredness. Christ turns nakedness into sacredness with His covering power. Christ is our sacredness.

V

THE WISDOM OF WARFARE

One of the main reasons we are spiritually and mentally weak is because we try to fight battles for which we are not spiritually and mentally prepared for, battles for which we lack the strength that we're unable to attain on our own. The reason we lack the strength to fight is because it is a spiritual battle, a spiritual war. We were born weak to spiritual things because we were born in sin and flesh. The flesh and the spirit are constantly at war. Apostle Paul wrote about this war between the flesh and the spirit in Galatians 5, which says:

> So I say, walk by the Spirit, and you will not gratify the desires of the flesh. For the flesh desires what is contrary to the Spirit, and the Spirit what is contrary to the flesh. They are in conflict with each other, so that you are not to do whatever you want. But

if you are led by the Spirit, you are not under the law. (Galatians 5:16–18 NIV)

There is a constant war between our flesh and spirit. The flesh wants to follow the things that lead to death. The Spirit wants to follow things of God and life. They hate each other. We're born in sin because of the curse of the flesh caused by Adam and Eve's disobedience to God's word.

Genesis 3 speaks of Adam and Eve's disobedience to God in the garden of Eden. Allow me to briefly explain the story. Adam was created from the dust of the earth. Eve was created from the rib of Adam. Adam and Eve were the first beings made in the image of God and were given dominion to rule the garden of Eden. The garden of Eden was a sacred place that God created for Adam and Eve to live with no worries or cares. Adam and Eve did not wear clothes because they were covered in God's glory. The couple oversaw taking care of the land, animals, and garden. The Lord gave Adam a single instruction about the garden. The Lord told Adam that he and Eve were allowed to eat of any tree of the Garden, but they could not eat of the tree of the knowledge of good and evil. This certain tree was forbidden to them, and God told them that if they ate of it, they would die because of their decision. So, we return to the text of Genesis chapter 3 with this back story. While Eve was working in the garden, a serpent began to talk to Eve about the tree of the knowledge of good and evil. Now, if you are like me, if a serpent slithered up to us and started talking, we would run away so fast there would be a trail of smoke behind us! But Eve was innocent, she did not know that it was strange for a serpent to talk. She was pure and easily deceived. The serpent began to question her about God's instruction. Genesis 3 records these events:

> Now the serpent was more crafty than any of the wild animals the Lord God had made. He said to the woman, "Did God really say, 'You must not eat from any tree in the garden'?" The woman said to the serpent, "We may eat fruit from the trees in the garden, but God did say, 'You must not eat fruit from the tree that is in the middle of the garden, and you must not touch it, or you will die.'" "You will not certainly die," the serpent said to the woman. "For God knows that when you eat from it your eyes will be opened, and you will be like God, knowing good and evil." (Genesis 3:1–5 NIV)

If you notice, the serpent didn't know God's direct instruction to Adam and Eve, so it questioned Eve to see if Eve would tell it about the true instruction from God. The serpent or Satan is crafty, not almighty, anything that he knows is because it was told to him, not because he knew it first. When Eve revealed the instruction, the serpent counterattacked by suggesting that they would not die and that their eyes were going to be opened to be like God as if God was holding back information from them. The serpent was disguising the suggestion of rebellion inside of the suggestion of enlightenment.

The enemy will always suggest that God's creation to turn away from God in a way where it looks like they are breaking away from a system. The enemy will always try to suggest an education that teaches us to try to be God and not to be with God. The serpent knows that we are the most powerful when we choose to be with God. When we choose to be with God, we can do all things that the enemy wants to limit us from doing. When we take the suggestion of being God, the enemy can control us with sin, addiction, money, and anything else that tries to compete with God. So now some try to compete with God instead of being complete with God. Genesis 3 continues:

> When the woman saw that the fruit of the tree was good for food and pleasing to the eye, and desirable for gaining wisdom, she took some and ate it. She also gave some to her husband, who was with her, and he ate it. Then the eyes of both of them were opened, and they realized

they were naked; so they sewed fig leaves together and made coverings for themselves. (Genesis 3:5–7 NIV)

Notice that when Adam and Eve's eyes were opened, they saw their own nakedness. When they took the serpent's suggestion, they lost their privilege of being covered in the glory of God. They didn't see themselves as gods, they saw themselves naked and without God. The enemy deceived them to trade God's glory for false enlightenment. They traded sacredness for nakedness. The glory of God departed from them and now they didn't see trust, but dust. They realized that they were not a part of God but apart from God, and they were ashamed and tied figs together to cover their nakedness. They became the first fashion designers ever, piecing together coverings to cover their shame. They used the plants of the garden God had given them to cover themselves where sacred places used to be. They were deceived and chose to search for what was already given to them. They chose rebellion and curse. They chose heartache and pain. They chose grief and anxiety. They chose sin and death.

The story goes on with Adam and Eve trying to hide themselves from God as God was walking through the garden:

Then the man and his wife heard the sound of the Lord God as he was walking in the garden in the cool of the day, and they hid from the Lord God among the trees of the garden. 9 But the Lord God called to the man, "Where are you?"

He answered, "I heard you in the garden, and I was afraid because I was naked; so I hid."

And he said, "Who told you that you were naked? Have you eaten from the tree that I commanded you not to eat from? (Gen. 3:8–11 NIV).

God knew that Adam and Eve had eaten from the tree before He called out for them, but Adam and Eve attempted to hide their nakedness from God. Adam and Eve attempted to cover themselves and hide because they understood they had disobeyed God and they realized that they were no longer covered in God's glory. God called out to them to give them the choice to answer for themselves.

God asked Adam and Eve two question:

1.) "Who told you that you were naked?"

2.) "Have you eaten from the tree that I have commanded you not to eat from?"

These two questions are pivotal in the lives of every human because both questions speak of two things that every human wrestles with. The first is image and the second is identity.

Adam and Eve were created in God's image, but because they disobeyed, they were ashamed of their image and tried to hide it from God. God created Adam and Eve's identity, but the serpent deceived them to believe that they did not need God's identification and chose to identify life for themselves. These caused Adam and Eve to fall short of the glory of God. The Bible says in Romans 3:23, "for all have sinned and come short of the glory of God," and Genesis 3 continues

> The man said, "The woman you put here with me—she gave me some fruit from the tree, and I ate it."
>
> Then the Lord God said to the woman, "What is this you have done?"
>
> The woman said, "The serpent deceived me, and I ate."
>
> So the Lord God said to the serpent, "Because you have done this,
>
> "Cursed are you above all livestock and all wild animals!
>
> You will crawl on your belly and you will eat dust all the days of your life. And I will put enmity between you and the woman, and between your offspring and hers; he

will crush your head, and you will strike his heel." (Genesis 3:12–15 NIV)

Adam instantly blamed the woman for giving him the fruit, after God gave Adam the instruction specifically. Adam attempted to play the blame game and not take responsibility because he'd lost his identity and covering. God placed a curse upon the serpent for deceiving Eve. The decision that Adam and Eve made to disobey God and to try to identify themselves without God brought a curse upon them and the grounds of the earth. So, the broken trust cursed the dust. God allowed a curse to come upon women because of Eve's actions. Genesis 3 continues:

> To the woman he said, "I will make your pains in childbearing very severe; with painful labor you will give birth to children. Your desire will be for your husband, and he will rule over you."

To Adam he said, "Because you listened to your wife and ate fruit from the tree about which I commanded you, 'You must not eat from it, "Cursed is the ground because of you; through painful toil you will eat food from it all the days of your life. It will produce thorns and thistles for you, and you will eat the plants of the field. By the sweat of your brow you will eat your food until you return to the ground, since from it you were taken; for dust you are and to dust you will return." (Genesis 3:16–19 NIV)

I want to explain the significance of God cursing the ground because of the disobedience of Adam. God did not curse the soul of mankind; God cursed the ground that man lived upon. God cursed the dust of the ground that whatever grew from the ground now had dominion over mankind instead of mankind having dominion over the ground. The ground was now cursed to work against them. Bushes would now grow thorns and thistles. Plants will now be choked by weeds. The earth was now an enemy of mankind. Because Adam was made from the dust of the earth, when God cursed the dust or the ground, it put man under a curse. Mankind's body or flesh is made of dust, so when God cursed the ground, He cursed our flesh. Now our flesh desires the things that make us rebel against God or try to be God and not with God. Our flesh is cursed. Our flesh seeks death. Our flesh seeks to return to the earth, while our spirit desires life and to see God glorified in the earth. Our souls need salvation so that we can receive the grace to follow the Spirit and not the flesh. Without salvation our soul automatically follows the things of the flesh because of the curse. But salvation puts the deeds of the flesh to death and awakens us in the Spirit so that we can follow the Spirit of God into life. First Peter 3:19 records, "For Christ also suffered once for sins, the righteous for the unrighteous, to bring you to God. He was put to death in the body but made alive in the Spirit."

This makes clear that salvation is only through Christ Jesus. Christ lived a perfect life. He did not sin. Christ is the Son of God. He is the Word of God. He is God, yet He still chose to sacrifice His life so that mankind could be saved from sin that controls the flesh, which leads to death. On the cross Christ's flesh was ripped and torn. He became a blood sacrifice for the sin of all of mankind, dying a death that He didn't deserve so He could break the curse that was over the ground of mankind. Christ broke the curse of the flesh, but we must choose to be free from the curse by choosing Him, believing that He lived, He died, and that God the Father raised Him from the dead. When we do this, we accept salvation. When we accept salvation, God covers our naked flesh with his sacred Glory. Accept and follow Christ. Commit your life to living the life that Christ lived and teaches us to live, and you will learn to live free of the flesh and to live free of the curse. Receive Him. Through Christ, the grief of sin transforms into the belief of grace.

When we receive salvation, we receive life in the Spirit. We live covered by the glory of God just like Adam and Eve did before they disobeyed. We are not naked in sin anymore; we are covered in grace. Every kingdom warrior needs this conversion because you must have life in the Spirit and have the discipline of following the Spirit so that you can win this spiritual war. You can't experience the victory of warfare until you enlist into the kingdom troop. You enlist by committing to Christ. God has taken the leaves of your shame that you used to cover yourself and has covered you in glory, and His glory comes with armor.

The Whole Armor

In this transformation process I want to explain how pivotal your armor is in battle. Your armor was created by God to shield you from the tactics of the enemy. The glory of God covers your nakedness, while the armor of God protects your sacredness. Apostle Paul urges the church of Ephesus to put on the whole armor of God to stand against the schemes of the devil. Ephesians 6 says:

> Finally, be strong in the Lord and in his mighty power. Put on the full armor of God, so that you can take your stand against the devil's schemes. For our struggle is not against flesh and blood, but against the rulers, against the authorities, against the powers of this dark world and against the spiritual forces of evil in the heavenly realms. (Ephesians 6:10–12 NIV)

Adam and Eve were naked and innocent towards the schemes of the devil, who deceived them out of the glory of God. The Holy Spirit has equipped us with armor that will protect us from falling into the schemes of the enemy and falling out of the glory of God. It is our choice to put on the armor. The armor was given to us as kingdom warriors so that we can be confident in standing against the attacks of the enemy. We are to be strong in the Lord and in His mighty power and not depend on our own strength to fight a spiritual battle. If we depend on our own strength, we will be devoured by the enemy because our flesh is not equipped to endure the devil's schemes, because our flesh is cursed to submit to the schemes of the devil. Our flesh desires the schemes of the devil. Depending on the power of the Lord's might and not your own, will tame the desires of the flesh and give confidence to our spirits to stand against the devil's schemes.

David wrote Psalm 18. He recognized that the Lord is the one who taught him how to be the fierce warrior that he was. David echoes New Testament scripture about the whole armor of God in Psalm 18, which reads:

> He teacheth my hands to war, so that a bow of steel is broken by mine arms. / Thou hast also given me the shield of thy salvation: and thy right hand hath holden me up, and thy gentleness hath made me great. / Thou hast enlarged my steps under me, that my feet did not slip. (Psalm 18:34–36 KJV)

David also wrote a similar song in Psalm 144, which records: "1 Praise be to the Lord my Rock, who trains my hands for war, my fingers for battle. / He is my loving God and my fortress, my stronghold and my deliverer, / my shield, in whom I take refuge, who subdues peoples under me" (Ps. 144:1–2 NIV).

This text reminds me of an earlier story of David found in 1 Samuel 17, which relates the classic story of David and Goliath. It is also the origin story of one of David's first encounters with King Saul. David was just a shepherd boy at the time and was commissioned by his father Jesse to bring lunch to his brothers who were fighting in war. David has already been anointed to be king but still worked in his father's field. David was an errand boy to his father, running his father's errands and taking care of his father's flock. David was sent to aid his brothers with food and drink not to participate in battle.

When David arrived with the food for his brothers, he saw his brothers and the army of Israel cowering before a giant champion warrior named Goliath. Goliath was openly challenging the troop to battle and blaspheming or disrespecting the God of Israel. First Samuel 17 says,

> As he was talking with them, Goliath, the Philistine champion from Gath, stepped out from his lines and shouted his usual defiance, and David heard it. Whenever the Israelites saw the man, they all fled

from him in great fear. Now the Israelites had been saying, "Do you see how this man keeps coming out? He comes out to defy Israel. The king will give great wealth to the man who kills him. He will also give him his daughter in marriage and will exempt his family from taxes in Israel." David asked the men standing near him, "What will be done for the man who kills this Philistine and removes this disgrace from Israel? Who is this uncircumcised Philistine that he should defy the armies of the living God?" (1 Samuel 17:23–26 NIV)

The disrespect of Goliath made David see blood. In his red-hot anger, he decided to call Goliath out for his blasphemous towards God and Israel. David had confidence in God to defeat Goliath although Goliath was feared by warriors who seemed greater than David. To the warriors, Goliath was a threat to Israel. To David, Goliath was a disgrace to Israel and an affront to his God. David was given boldness by God to not be threatened by Goliath, but to be aggravated into battle by Goliath. God used David's aggravation to fuel David's confidence in Him.

The army of Israel was sorely afraid of Goliath, but David was aggravated by the lack of heart that Israel had for God in this encounter. David looked at Goliath as an embarrassment to Israel, but David's brother Eliab looked at David as an embarrassment for giving voice on this matter. First Samuel 17 records:

> When Eliab, David's oldest brother, heard him speaking with the men, he burned with anger at him and asked, "Why have you come down here? And with whom did you leave those few sheep in the wilderness? I know how conceited you are and how wicked your heart is; you came down only to watch the battle. "Now what have I done?" said David. "Can't I even speak?" He then turned away to someone else and brought up the same matter, and the men answered him as before. What David said was overheard and reported to Saul, and Saul sent for him. (1 Samuel 17:28–31 NIV)

David was appalled by the lack of bravery in the army of Israel. Eliab insulted his brother but that did not stop David from voicing his bravery against Goliath to the men of Israel.

I want to address those of you who were counted out and restricted by what people have told you who they thought you were. What people said you were and what God created you to be are totally different. When family members, neighbors, friends, coworkers, or even loved ones limit us with their perceptions of who they think we are, it sometimes hinders us and restricts us from doing and being what God has called us to do and be. It really hurts when the people who are the closest to us don't expect much from us. If we allow it to, this belief will restrict us. We will end up living in other people's idea of who we are instead of living in God's identity for our lives. We will become slaves to their perception, and it hinders our function and obedience to instructions. Sometimes we dumb ourselves down because we are so afraid of what our restrictors will say about what God has called us to do.

We must ask the Holy Spirit for boldness to stand against the lies of the enemy that flows through the mouths of those who don't understand who we really are. David's brother belittled David for just being a shepherd boy and questioned his ability and motive. David boldly stood against his brother by standing in the boldness that God was supplying for him to fight Goliath. He didn't respond to the comments of his brother, he responded to the commitment to his God.

Stop trying to think of comebacks against your restrictors. You are wasting your words and your time because there is a giant that needs to be slain and the defiant words come to distract you. Don't let defiance distract you from killing the giant. Silence the defiance with your obedience to God. You have nothing to prove to naysayers. The truth is, when you are standing in obedience to God, they are coming against God and not you. Stop trying to prove to your restrictors who you are. You are not going to say something that's going to change their minds about you. God is going to do something that is going to change their minds about you. They don't not hold your identity, God does.

The Spirit of God moved David to action, "David said to Saul, 'Let no one lose heart on account of this Philistine; your servant will go and fight him" (1 Sam. 17:32 NIV). Everyone laughed because David was a young, small boy at the time. They looked at David's attempt to fight Goliath as cute. David was still persistent about killing Goliath.

King Saul was not convinced that a boy like David could take out one of the largest champion warriors of the Philistine army. David was eager to kill Goliath, and he told King Saul about a time when he'd killed a lion and a bear for trying to attack his father's flock of sheep. Somehow the story convinced King Saul to let David fight as we see in this scripture, "The Lord who rescued me from the paw of the lion and the paw of the bear will rescue me from the hand of this Philistine. Saul said to David, "Go, and the Lord be with you" (1 Sam. 17:37).

This part of the story about David and Goliath is the most important part of this story in this chapter of the book about warfare and the whole armor of God. First Samuel 17 says:

> Then Saul dressed David in his own tunic. He put a coat of armor on him and a bronze helmet on his head. David fastened on his sword over the tunic and tried walking around, because he was not used to them. "I cannot go in these," he said to Saul, "because I am not used to them." So he took them off. (1 Samuel 17:38–39 NIV)

David knew that King Saul's armor was not the right fit for him and it would be a hindrance for David. David could not trust the king of Israel's armor because he was not trained to use it. David was trained to use the King of King's armor. David was empowered by the Spirit of the Lord to kill the lion and the bear. David understood that he needed to be empowered by the Spirit of the Lord to defeat Goliath, and to be empowered by God for the task, he had to deny the armor of the flesh and embrace the armor of the Spirit.

In the account of First Samuel 17, as David approached Goliath, Goliath began to taunt David's size, stature, and ability,

> He looked David over and saw that he was little more than a boy, glowing with health and handsome, and he despised him. He said to David, "Am I a dog,

that you come at me with sticks?" And the Philistine cursed David by his gods. "Come here," he said, "and I'll give your flesh to the birds and the wild animals." (1 Samuel 17:42–44)

David was not afraid of the insults and the judgment of Goliath. David knew his God. Goliath was not a threat to David; David was a threat to Goliath. David's humiliation displayed by Goliath was an entryway for God to show great power through David. Although Goliath sized David up to be just a boy, David knew the size of his God. David had seen God deliver through him before and he had confidence that God would do it again. This was the greatest armor that David had. David's armor was his trust in the Lord and the power of His name. First Samuel 17 records:

> David said to the Philistine, "You come against me with sword and spear and javelin, but I come against you in the name of the Lord Almighty, the God of the armies of Israel, whom you have defied. This day the Lord will deliver you into my hands, and I'll strike you down and cut off your head. This very day I will give the carcasses of the Philistine army to the birds and the wild animals, and the whole world

will know that there is a God in Israel. All those gathered here will know that it is not by sword or spear that the Lord saves; for the battle is the Lord's, and he will give all of you into our hands." (1 Samuel 17:45–47 NIV)

David had the greatest armor in Israel, the name of the Lord. David understood the power of the name of the Lord Almighty. If David would've used King Saul's armor, King Saul would've taken credit for what only the Spirit of the Lord can do. David had to come in the name of the Lord so that the Spirit of God could take over David and do the work that David was proclaiming to Goliath. The Lord would use David's reverence to take the head of Goliath and bring glory to His name. First Samuel 17:

> As the Philistine moved closer to attack him, David ran quickly toward the battle line to meet him. Reaching into his bag and taking out a stone, he slung it and struck the Philistine on the forehead. The stone sank into his forehead, and he fell face down on the ground. So David triumphed over the Philistine with a sling and a stone; without a sword in his hand, he struck down the Philistine and killed him. David ran and stood over him. He

took hold of the Philistine's sword and drew it from the sheath. After he killed him, he cut off his head with the sword. When the Philistines saw that their hero was dead, they turned and ran. (1 Samuel 17:48–51 NIV)

David's armor wasn't physical armor that every other warrior was wearing. His armor was the name of the Lord, and his power was the Spirit of the living God. David defeated Goliath in the name of the Lord, not in the name of Israel. If He would have used Israel's name, he would have to depend on the fighting skills of Israel. David came in the name of the Lord, so he depended on the might of the Lord. The might of the Lord will always win.

I want to address you for a moment. Whose name are you coming in? Whose name are you fighting in? Whose power are you drawing from in this spiritual battle? Whose armor are you trying to fit? Some of us are fighting battles with fighting styles and armor that were created by our past oppressors. Some of us are trying to fight this war with armor that abusive parents gave us. Some of us have fighting skills that bad habits have taught us. Some of us are still coming into this spiritual conflict in the name of our abusers. We pull from the strength of bad examples instead of the supernatural power of God. That's why we are losing the fight; we can't win without the might of the Spirit of God. We try to fight with our cultural backgrounds, we even try to use our education and occupations to fight. We try to come in our own name. Those things cannot help you in a spiritual battle. The battle between David and Goliath proved to be a spiritual battle more than a physical battle. Their face-off was not natural, it was supernatural. I want to tell you the same thing, your battle is not natural but supernatural. You need a supernatural empowerment from the everlasting God to win this supernatural battle or war. It's time for you to drop every other name and depend solely on the name of the Lord and His power. The name of the Lord guarantees victory. When you come in His name, you come in His victory.

The name of the Lord gave David a confidence to fight, because it was a name that was greater than his. David's fighting posture was not in who he was but in who his God is. David was able to fight in the supernatural because he had the right posture. The right posture holds confidence. A person who has confidence doesn't drop their heads and back out in defeat but stands tall with their chest out because they are confident in who they are. Supernaturally, the right posture is not in the "who I am," but in the "great I Am." Your posture is sure because you know who you belong to, which will organically define who you are. The name of the Lord will name those who walk in the name of the Lord.

Recall the moment when Moses met God as the burning bush in Exodus 3. God assigned Moses to go to Egypt and tell the Egyptians and Pharaoh to let the Israelites free from slavery. Moses was terrified to go and speak because he had a speech problem and he left Egypt because he had killed someone. Going to speak against the city he grew up in and was running from was terrifying, especially for someone who had no confidence in their ability to speak and lead. Moses was looking at his situation more from the perspective of "who I am" than trusting in the great *I Am* posture. Exodus 3 says:

> But Moses said to God, "Who am I that I should go to Pharaoh and bring the Israelites out of Egypt?" And God said, "I will be with you. And this will be the sign to you that it is I who have sent you: When you have brought the people out of Egypt, you will worship God on this mountain." Moses said to God, "Suppose I go to the Israelites and say to them, 'The God of your fathers has sent me to you,' and they ask me, 'What is his name?' Then what shall I tell them?" God said to Moses, "I Am Who I Am. This is what you are to say to the Israelites: 'I Am has sent me to you.'" (Exodus 3:11–14 NIV)

God wanted Moses to shift his dependance off his own abilities and totally depend on the Lord. God did not want Moses's ability, God wanted Moses's availability. God was set to put periods where Moses had question marks. God changed Moses's own "who am I?" into God's "Who I Am." God converted Moses's mindset from his own name of "I am what I am" into God's name of "I Am Who I Am." Moses was able to go to Egypt and do all that God said because he stood and obeyed the Lord with confidence in the name of the Lord. David, Moses, and others in biblical context, who encountered the Spirit of the Lord didn't know that the Spirit of the Lord was God's Son, Jesus the Christ. Jesus is the name of the Lord hidden from those in the Old Testament and revealed to those in the New Testament. Jesus is the name of the Lord and Jesus is the Lord. When we stand confident in who Jesus is and not in who we are, we stand, proclaim, and perform the mighty works of the Lord.

Proverbs 18:10 records: "The name of the Lord is a fortified tower; the righteous run to it and are safe."

Your Stand Is Your Fight

In this transformation process, it is important that you learn how to wear your armor and use your weapon. Your armor is not physical armor. Physical armor is just dust in the spiritual realm. You need something stronger, something supernatural. Jesus gives all His kingdom warriors, spiritual armor and weapons so they will be well equipped in battle. God did not give us the armor so that we can fight, but so we can stand. Let me explain. Ephesians 6:13 records: "Therefore put on the full armor of God, so that when the day of evil comes, you may be able to stand your ground, and after you have done everything, to stand."

In the realm of spiritual conflict, standing your ground activates the power of God to fight in a situation. Standing your ground does more damage to the kingdom of darkness than throwing a fist or slinging a sword could ever do. God uses our kingdom stance to resist the enemy's schemes and plots. If we stand our ground, we don't have to lift a finger, our standing will defeat the enemy. God will fight through us when we stand our ground for Him.

Adam and Eve didn't stand their ground when the serpent deceived them. If they would have stood their ground on what God instructed them to do, they would have resisted the enemy. Instead, they gave in to temptation. Their failure to stand their ground gave the ground dominion over them instead of them having dominion over the ground. They were meant to stand on top of the ground but now the ground would stand on top of them.

What is your stance? Is your stance to be obedient no matter what or do you let your stance be broken because of the evil that you face? Are you standing on top of your ground or is your ground standing on top of you? It's territorial when you cover your ground. It's burial when your ground covers you.

When you stand with the armor of God, the enemy is automatically defeated. Your armor is enemy repellant. Your armor was made by God to resist the enemy. Your armor fights while you stand. When you stand against the enemy, the Lord will fight through your armor. Your stance builds resistance against the enemy. When you stand your ground, the Lord commands your ground. Standing is resisting. James 4:7 says, "Submit yourselves, then, to God. Resist the devil, and he will flee from you."

I am going to take the time to teach you what your armor is according to the Word of God and how to use it in the war that you are facing as a kingdom warrior. There are specific pieces of armor with specific capabilities that will help you as you stand against the enemy. I will give the names of the pieces of armor and explain the functions of the pieces of armor given to cover us so we can stand against the devil's schemes. Ephesians 6 records:

> Stand firm then, with the belt of truth buckled around your waist, with the breastplate of righteousness in place, and with your feet fitted with the readiness that comes from the gospel of peace. In addition to all this, take up the shield of faith, with which you can extinguish all the flaming arrows of the evil one. Take the helmet of salvation and the sword

of the Spirit, which is the word of God. (Ephesian 6:14–17 NIV)

1.) Belt of Truth

The definition of truth is the quality or state of being true. As kingdom warriors, God's truth should always be tightened around our bodies. Our armor should be fastened with the truth. When we are fastened together by God's truth, we will not fall apart when we are hit with the enemy's lies.

What are God's truths? God's truths are the decrees and commands that God has set from the beginning of time for His creation to follow. The truth of God is the absolute truth. The absolute truth is that the Lord is the only true and living God. God is the only God who ever was, who is, and is to come. The truth is that in God there is no sin and darkness, and that mankind must be pure from sin to be in right standing with God the Father.

The truth is that no sin shall go unpunished in God's sight. The wages of sin is death, but the gift of God is eternal life (Rom. 6:23). The ultimate truth is that God is love. God loved the world so much that He gave His only begotten Son and if you believe in Him, you will not perish but have everlasting life (John 3:16). Jesus is God's Son who came to redeem mankind from sin and to destroy the works of the devil (1 John 3:8). Whoever believes in His Son pleases God the Father and will be saved from God's wrath against the kingdom of darkness and wickedness. The truth is that when we accept Jesus, God the Father pardons us from all our sins and shortcomings.

The truth is Jesus is the Word of God, the Lamb of God, and that He is God. The love of God snatches us out of rebellion, sin, and hell. The absolute truth is that Christ will return one day to gather His people (the church) and bring justice against the devil and his wicked followers once and for all. God will then make a new heaven and earth, free from sin and wickedness for Him and His people to dwell as one (Rev. 21).

We must believe the absolute truth and allow this truth to fasten our armor so that we can stand in truth and not give in to the devil's deceit. Believe God's truth and let the belt of God's truth fasten your armor. Be fastened in God's truth.

2.) Breastplate of Righteousness

Righteousness is the quality of being morally right or justifiable. Kingdom warriors should always uphold the truth that we cannot obtain righteousness on our own. There is nothing that we can do to justify us as righteous in the eyes of God. Our righteousness is like filthy rags (Isa. 4:6). We are sinful beings, nothing we do can achieve righteousness in God's eyes. Abram, also known as Abraham, was the earthly father of faith. Abram was a pagan who served others' gods before following God and putting his faith in the Lord God's commands. Abram was not righteous before believing in the Lord God. His belief in the Lord is what made him righteous unto the Lord God (Gen. 15:6). It was Abram's belief that was righteous because it is the Lord who is righteous. Jesus is the fulfillment of righteousness. Abraham put his belief in the Lord God, the Lord God was Jesus in the Old Testament before Christ was born into the world.

John 8:56 sys, "Your father Abraham rejoiced to see my day, and he saw it and was glad."

Jesus was and is the Word of God. The Word of God was made flesh and came to earth to bring righteousness to mankind. Christ is the only righteous one God the Father deems to be righteous. The only way that we can achieve righteousness is by surrendering to Christ. What Christ did on the cross absolved all mankind of sin even though we don't deserve it. We can't do anything that overachieves what Christ has done. Christ's birth, life, suffering, death, and resurrection pardon us from our sins and redeemed us to right standing with God. The breastplate of righteousness is a protection for the heart against the evils of the enemy and a badge of humility that protects us from self-righteousness, which is the exaltation of actions that people believe makes them righteous.

Self-righteousness is a form of pride that tries to compete with the life and sacrifice of Christ Jesus. Although this is strong language, God looks at self-righteousness like a woman's garment that is stained with period blood. God looks at our attempts to achieve righteousness as worthless because Christ already achieved the righteousness that we are striving to obtain. Self- righteousness has started beliefs and religions that exalt themselves against God. God is the only One who can call someone righteous. God the Father is the Creator of all things. He knows the standard of what He created. God created the standard of righteousness. Jesus is the standard. Jesus is righteousness.

We cannot obtain righteousness without Christ. Through Christ we become righteousness (2 Cor. 5:20–21). As kingdom warriors we should keep the breastplate of righteousness in place so that we can uphold the standard of righteousness that Christ has set for His kingdom to stand in.

3.) Feet Prepared with the Gospel of Peace

The earthly definition of peace is freedom from disturbance, tranquility. The spiritual definition of peace is freedom in disturbance. Earthly peace gives off a sense of escape to those who are in trouble. God's peace is a promise of escape during trouble. Earthly peace gives a sense of removal from trouble. God's peace gives the way of escape in trouble. Earthly peace discards but God's peace guards. Philippians 4 records: "Be careful for nothing; but in every thing by prayer and supplication with thanksgiving let your requests be made known unto God. And the peace of God, which passeth all understanding, shall keep your hearts and minds through Christ Jesus." (Phil. 4:6–7 KJV).

God's peace will guard you in the middle of the war, and it will guide your feet. As kingdom warriors we must stay prepared to stand in God's peace. For us to obtain the peace of God we must obtain peace with God. Christ was and is the atonement. We were rebellious in our sins, which made us enemies of God. Through Christ Jesus and His willingness to sacrifice His own life to make us children of God, we now can obtain peace with God. We can only obtain peace with God through faith in Christ Jesus. Christ Jesus is the place where we meet with and find peace with our Heavenly Father. We must accept Christ as our Lord and Savior and believe that He is the Son God. When we confess Jesus, it gives us peace with God the Father. Romans 10 records: "That if thou shalt confess with thy mouth the Lord Jesus, and shalt believe in thine heart that God hath raised him from the dead, thou shalt be saved. For with the heart man believeth unto righteousness; and with the mouth confession is made unto salvation" (Rom. 10:9–10 KJV).

Our belief in Christ gives us access to the peace of God.

4.) Shield of Faith

Faith is complete trust or confidence in someone or something. Faith is a confidence that is complete. Faith is not confirmed by evidence or facts but rather faith is our response to whatever God has told us to do. Faith is the willingness to step out on what you were told by God. The faith that you step out in will give you the power to stand behind it as well. You cannot have faith in something that God did not say.

Romans 10:17 says, "So then faith cometh by hearing, and hearing by the word of God."

Faith in God will shield us from putting confidence in ourselves alone and from any doubt that the victory belongs to the children of God in any situation or tribulation. The Word says that the shield of faith will extinguish the flaming arrows of the enemy. Faith is not only a response to God's word but also a defense against the enemy's attack. When you have faith in the God of heaven and earth, your faith becomes a shield to defend you against the attacks of the devil. Your faith activates the hand of God and the heart of God in your tribulation. When you have complete confidence in God, you have something to stand behind when the darts of the enemy are flinging towards you as fast as bullets. When doubt, discouragement, disease, struggles, and discontent come, your faith in God will become a shield to make you stand in confidence against the devil's attempts to destroy you.

Hebrews 11:6 says, "But without faith it is impossible to please him: for he that cometh to God must believe that he is, and that he is a rewarder of them that diligently seek him."

Faith pleases God, but many people lack the faith that God is looking for. Complete confidence in God moves the heart of God to urgently act on your behalf. God will reward you with the victory in what you are believing and standing for when you exhibit complete confidence in Him.

The shield of faith lets you stand behind your faith in the Lord, and when you stand behind your faith in God, your faith will defend you against the many doubts and attacks from the enemy.

5.) Helmet of Salvation

The definition of salvation is preservation or deliverance from harm, ruin, or loss. Salvation is not earned, it's a gift. The salvation of the Lord restores the loss. The salvation of the Lord transforms savages into saints. Before Christ died on the cross for our sins, we were subject to sin, death, and hell. Mankind lived their lives in subjection to sin and rebellion. Some lived very wicked lives before Christ salvaged them from the ruins of sin. When Jesus gave His life on the cross, He purchased us from sin, death, and hell. Now we are no longer separated from God and lost in sin. We have been salvaged from sin and the wrath of God by Christ. There is transformation in the salvation of the Lord. We must put on the helmet of salvation so that we can keep our minds in a posture of transformation.

The helmet of salvation protects our minds. Our minds need to be salvaged every day because the mind grows wild and is subject to sin every day when the mind is not subjected to salvation every day. The helmet of salvation transforms the mind and tames it so it can think the thoughts of Christ and not of rebellion.

A real helmet of salvation doesn't look like a prestigious head covering that a warrior uses to shield their heads; it looks like a crown of thorns. Let us read about Jesus's helmet of salvation, His crown of thorns. John 19 records:

> Then Pilate therefore took Jesus, and scourged him. And the soldiers platted a crown of thorns, and put it on his head, and they put on him a purple robe, And said, Hail, King of the Jews! and they smote him with their hands. Pilate therefore went forth again, and saith unto them, Behold, I bring him forth to you, that ye may know that I find no fault in him. Then came Jesus forth, wearing the crown of thorns, and the purple robe. And Pilate saith unto them, Behold the man! When the chief priests therefore and officers saw him, they cried out, saying, Crucify him, crucify him. Pilate saith unto them, Take

ye him, and crucify him: for I find no fault
in him." (John 19:1–6 KJV)

Here we see our savior Christ Jesus receiving a purple robe and a crown of thorns as mockery. Let's focus on the crown of thorns. The crown of thorns was braided together and shoved into the Lord's head as mockery of His kingship and kingdom. The crown of thorns was meant to be physical mockery but represented spiritual victory. If there had not been a crown of thorns braided for Jesus the Christ's head, there would be no salvation for the mind. See, the crown of thorns pierced through Christ's head, pierced his brain, which signified Christ restoring the brain and renewing the mind of mankind. The crown of thorns represents restoration for the mind. Without the crown of thorns, there would be no crucifixion of the old brain and mind. When Christ took the crown of thorns, it salvaged the minds of all who believe. When we choose Christ and we take the helmet of salvation, it crucifies our minds and renews our minds to have the mind of Christ Jesus. The helmet of salvation and the crown of thorns are the same.

The helmet of salvation will keep your mind from thinking in sinful nature. The helmet of salvation transforms the nature of the fallen mind and activates the nature of Christ's mind in our own. The helmet of salvation gives you sober and holy thoughts. It also protects the peace of mind that the salvation of the Lord gives. The helmet of salvation is a symbol of re-creation.

As kingdom warriors we should daily put on the helmet of salvation, so that our minds can be renewed daily. It is not good for a kingdom warrior to stand in a kingdom battle with a sinful mentality. If a kingdom warrior tries to fight with a sinful and wild mentality, they will not endure the sound instructions of the Holy Spirit. They will not subject themselves to the commands of the Lord while in battle but will try to take matters in their own hands. This mentality works against the kingdom of God. When you don't think with a crucified mentality, you will betray the kingdom to follow your own personal efforts in the battle.

Not crucifying the mind daily will also lead us back to a sinful lifestyle. We are fast to conform to this world when we don't allow the helmet of salvation to renew our minds. Romans 12:2 records: "And be not conformed to this world: but be ye transformed by the renewing of your mind, that ye may prove what is that good, and acceptable, and perfect, will of God."

It is the will of God for the kingdom to be transformed by the renewing of our minds, so that we can think like Christ in the middle of this daily kingdom war with darkness. Renewing our minds in the salvation of the Lord will keep darkness from controlling our minds. The helmet of salvation will crucify our sinful minds and flesh and bring the light and life of Christ to our minds daily.

6.) Sword of the Spirit

Ephesians 6:17 records: "Take the helmet of salvation and the sword of the Spirit, which is the word of God."

The Sword of the Spirit is the Word of God, which slices and dices all the attempts of the enemy to break the stance of kingdom warriors. God holds His Word higher than anything, and the Word of God is the sharpest weapon that a kingdom warrior has.

The Word of God is alive and active. Sharper than any double-edged sword, it penetrates even to dividing soul and spirit, joints and marrow; it judges the thoughts and attitudes of the heart (Heb. 4:12 NLT).

The Word of God cuts down wickedness and divides the wicked from the righteous. The Word of God separates darkness from light. In the beginning God's word created heaven, earth, and all of creation. Through the word of God, the waters were divided from the waters, day was divided from night, the light was divided from night, and the first created man was divided by God to create a woman. The word of God divided good and evil. Jesus was at the beginning with God the Father, Jesus is the Word that God sent out to create man (John 1). In Matthew 10: 34 Jesus proclaims: "Do not suppose that I have come to bring peace to the earth. I did not come to bring peace, but a sword."

The sword of the Spirit pierces through any unrighteous conjoined entity that the word of God does not validate or approve. Obtaining the sword of the Spirit is not just about reading your Bible (even though that is important). Obtaining the sword of the Spirit is allowing the Word of God to pierce your heart and cut away anything in your way and in your life that doesn't match up with His ordained word. Let the Word of God do work in your life. Let the Word of God cut away anything that is not of God in your life.

The sword of the Spirit slashes through anything that God's Word has not called to be. God created the heavens and earth with the sharpness of the Word. The Word of God has now been given to us as a weapon against the flesh and a sharpening tool for our spirit. As kingdom warriors, the sword of the Spirit should sharpen our spirits, and it will slash through any adversity that exalts itself against God and His kingdom.

Revelation 19 says this about Jesus's return: "And out of his mouth goeth a sharp sword, that with it he should smite the nations: and he shall rule them with a rod of iron: and he treadeth the winepress of the fierceness and wrath of Almighty God" (Rev. 19:15 KJV).

The Lord's tongue is a sharp sword when He returns to bring havoc and wrath to the kingdom of darkness and wicked kingdoms of this earth. The Lord's tongue shows us the sharpness of the Word of God. How Christ will sharply judge the world and sharply rescue His people.

The sword is a tool of creation for the righteous and a weapon of destruction towards the wicked. As a kingdom warrior, the sword of the Spirit is a necessity when standing against the power of darkness. The sword of the Spirit will pierce through the darkness, and the Word of the Lord will pierce through the hearts of men. The sword of the Spirit is the Word of God.

VI

EMERGE STRATEGICALLY

I want us to return to the life of David and the 400 men for most of this chapter. We thoroughly examined 1 Samuel 22:1–2. These specific scriptures were the initiation to the grand perspective of how God transforms weaklings into warriors, and I intentionally used these two scriptures to show the before, during, and after process of the transformation of the 400. Throughout the foregoing chapters we've explained the before process. God has given us revelation about the hidden during the process of the transformation. But now it is time to discuss and explain the after process of the transformation. I want to start off by explaining the after story of David and the 400 and march us forward to scriptures describing the amazing military exploits of David and his clan of fresh warriors.

Chapters 22 and 23 of 1 Samuel are the chapters that we will be examining for this discussion. First, let's do a quick review: David, the son of Jesse, is on the run for his life from King Saul of Israel; David serves King Saul as the leader of his troops; King Saul becomes jealous of David because God chose David to be the next king of Israel and has rejected Saul as King because of his disobedience to God. God allowed evil spirits to torment Saul, so Saul would lash out and try to kill David. Jonathan, the son of King Saul, warned David to run away because King Saul was determined to kill David. After a special sign was given to David that the death threat was true, David ran for his life.

After a series of events, David interacts with Ahimelek the priest and hides himself in the cave of Adullam. While hiding in the cave, David's family came to see him after hearing about his hiding place in the cave. Altogether, about 400 other people who were in despair, discouraged, and disheartened looked to David for leadership and came to be with David in the cave.

As we march forward in 1 Samuel 22:3–20, we see that David has gathered up his newly trained warriors. They went to Mizpah in Moab and made an agreement with the king to let David's family stay in Moab while David was in hiding. The prophet Gad gives David a prophecy that David should not stay in the stronghold or hiding place but go to the land of Judah, so David left and went to the forest of Horesh. King Saul learned where David and his men were hiding and began to announce his distrust for his officials

First Samuel 22 reports:

Now Saul heard that David and his men had been discovered. And Saul was seated, spear in hand, under the tamarisk tree on the hill at Gibeah, with all his officials standing at his side. He said to them, "Listen, men of Benjamin! Will the son of Jesse give all of you fields and vineyards? Will he make all of you commanders of thousands and commanders of hundreds? Is that why you have all conspired against me? No one tells me when my son makes a covenant with the son of Jesse. None of you is concerned about me or tells me that my son has incited my servant to lie in wait for me, as he does today. (1 Samuel 22:6–8 NIV)

Doeg the Edomite, one of King Saul's officials, stated to King Saul that he saw David speaking with Ahimelek and that Ahimelek fed David something to eat and offered him the sword of Goliath. King Saul summons Ahimelek the priest before him.

First Samuel 22 records:

> Then the king sent for the priest Ahimelek son of Ahitub and all the men of his family, who were the priests at Nob, and they all came to the king. Saul said, "Listen

now, son of Ahitub." "Yes, my lord," he answered. Saul said to him, "Why have you conspired against me, you and the son of Jesse, giving him bread and a sword and inquiring of God for him, so that he has rebelled against me and lies in wait for me, as he does today?

Ahimelek answered the king, "Who of all your servants is as loyal as David, the king's son-in-law, captain of your bodyguard and highly respected in your household? Was that day the first time I inquired of God for him? Of course not! Let not the king accuse your servant or any of his father's family, for your servant knows nothing at all about this whole affair." But the king said, "You will surely die, Ahimelek, you and your whole family." Then the king ordered the guards at his side: "Turn and kill the priests of the Lord, because they too have sided with David. They knew he was fleeing, yet they did not tell me." But the king's officials were unwilling to raise a hand to strike the priests of the Lord. The king then ordered Doeg, "You turn and strike down the priests." So Doeg the Edomite turned and struck them down.

That day he killed eighty-five men who wore the linen ephod. He also put to the sword Nob, the town of the priests, with its men and women, its children and infants, and its cattle, donkeys, and sheep. (1 Samuel 22:11–19 NIV)

Saul ordered that Ahimelek and his family be killed because they had aided David in his despair. Saul commanded his officials to kill Ahimelek the priest and all the priests of Israel, but they did not want to strike the Lord's priest. King Saul commanded Doeg the Edomite to kill the priest and he killed 85 priests including Ahimelek. One of Ahimelek's sons, Abiathar, fled and found David and joined his command.

First Samuel 22 continues the story, "Then David said to Abiathar, "That day, when Doeg the Edomite was there, I knew he would be sure to tell Saul. I am responsible for the death of your whole family. Stay with me; don't be afraid. The man who wants to kill you is trying to kill me too. You will be safe with me" (1 Sam. 22:22–23 NIV).

The scripture said that King Saul relentlessly searched for David but could not find him because the Lord hid David. David, with a troop behind him, was now running away from King Saul. We previously read that David and his troops defeated the Philistines in Keilah, so why was David and the troops running from King Saul? Couldn't

God deliver King Saul and his army into David's hands just like all the other tribes and armies?

Of course, God could have, but He never released David to fight King Saul but helped him to stay away from King Saul. God tasked David to show honor to King Saul although King Saul wanted to harm him. By causing David to run away, God was simply having mercy on King Saul because David had the favor from God to defeat King Saul. David is running from Saul to spare Saul's life and not his own. God was allowing David to hide from dishonor. God was giving honor to David and mercy to King Saul in a place where King Saul wanted honor and David wanted mercy. David and his family were used to running from King Saul out of fear, not knowing that God used David's running to shift David's place of hiding.

Every time King Saul would try to kill David after finding out where David was, he forced David to leave his place of hiding. David's mindset was not that he was sparing King Saul; David was legitimately scared of King Saul. God used David's confused fear to have mercy on Saul. God could've lifted His hand of mercy off Saul at any time and used David and his troops to destroy King Saul and his army. But God is merciful. There is a moment of mercy when David spared King Saul in 1 Samuel chapter 24 that we will dive into later. David's hiding was a strategic plan designed by God.

Give me a moment to address you. It is perfectly fine if you are not ready. Your development is strategically designed by God. Your maturity is not timed by the demands of others but by the commands of God. There is a purpose in your hiding. There is a purpose in your running. God is not hiding your development from the public because you're not ready, God is hiding you from the public because they are not ready for you. God has an appointed time to reveal you. In this new development you must emerge strategically. You must stay in the timing of God so you can arrive in God's time. You are going to learn something new about God and yourself in every hiding place that God leads you to run into. The things that God is revealing to you, in you, and through you cannot be revealed until God's perfect timing

It is a dangerous thing to reveal your hiding place to your enemies. We have a bad habit of allowing our hiding places to be revealed. God never lets a hiding place be revealed that He doesn't intend on migrating you from. God shifts our hiding places so that He can continue to use the ones He is hiding to carry out His will. God allows enemies to pursue the ones that God is hiding to get the ones He is hiding to move. My friend, God wants us to move. God does not want us to stay complacent in a certain phase or place.

God allows threats to cause migration. God uses treacheries to change trajectories. God uses the threats of our enemies to get us to move into promised places and uses our running to different hiding places to lure in our enemies to see His great power through us at an appointed time. Your running is confusing your enemies. They can't find you. Right now, your mentality is ready for your atmosphere but, your atmosphere is not ready for you. God is hiding you on purpose. God wants to reveal *you*, not your hiding places. He will always hide you.

Cut the Theatrics

By theatrics I mean excessively emotional and dramatic behavior. Sometimes we put ourselves in the category of "pretenders" because we long to put on a performance for people so that they can think we are something or somebody of value. God is not interested in actors in the kingdom. I'm not talking about the abilities and the gifts of a thespian who pretends to be a character because of a professional career. This has nothing to do with cinema or the arts. I'm not speaking of profession, but confession. This has everything to do with stance. Some of us are so used to putting on a show for others so that we can receive validation. Attempting to receive validation from others causes us to lose validity. God is not pleased when we pretend to be what we think people are satisfied by. We often put satisfaction over sanctification. We'd rather feel a part of the crowd than to be set apart from the crowd. We go out of our way to put on a theatrical performance for others so that others will accept us instead of being authentic with God even if others don't approve. Sometimes, we can be overly emotional, talkative, performance driven, and expressive so we can display to others a need for acceptance. We don't know how to not be seen because our identities revolve around what others see and say about us. God is not pleased with this mentality. Rejected places don't belong to people, rejected places belong to God. Your rejection is His protection. Rejected places are reserved places for God where He can speak to us and through us. Rejected places are not places of performance but rather places of private fellowship with God.

God is developing you not so you can be a good character, but so you can have good character. God is not leading us to give a good performance, but to give good obedience to Him (2 Tim. 2:15). Sometimes, we give others a boisterous performance but won't give God the Father the same energy. Although God doesn't require our self-righteous performances, He does require our devotional obedience. God is developing godly character in you, not so you can be seen, but so He can be seen. When we attempt to be a character that others can see, it's a place of pride that attempts to receive validation. When we display good character so that God can be seen, we are already validated by God. His validation is our identity, not the validation of others. Jesus speaks about people who attempt to perform to be seen in public using godly things. He calls them hypocrites. He is more drawn to those who live in private devotion to Him. He will use our private devotion in public to bring glory wherever

He is displaying the character He is displaying through us. Matthew 6 records His caution:

> "Be careful not to practice your righteousness in front of others to be seen by them. If you do, you will have no reward from your Father in heaven. "So when you give to the needy, do not announce it with trumpets, as the hypocrites do in the synagogues and on the streets, to be honored by others. Truly I tell you, they have received their reward in full.3 But when you give to the needy, do not let your left hand know what your right hand is doing, so that your giving may be in secret. Then your Father, who sees what is done in secret, will reward you. "And when you pray, do not be like the hypocrites, for they love to pray standing in the synagogues and on the street corners to be seen by others. Truly I tell you, they have received their reward in full. But when you pray, go into your room, close the door and pray to your Father, who is unseen. Then your Father, who sees what is done in secret, will reward you. And when you pray, do not keep on babbling like pagans, for they think they will be heard because of their

many words. Do not be like them, for your
Father knows what you need before you
ask him. (Matthew 6:1–8 NIV)

When I go to different Christian places of worship, the Holy Spirit leads me to observe the room. During the worship portion of the service, I sometimes see people kneeling, bowing, and crying in worship as the presence of God is pouring out. The presence of God is so strong at times, it causes some to burst out in emotion by running, shouting, and yelling praises to the Father. Although they are in public, these people are in a private place with God. It is such a beautiful experience.

The Holy Spirit also allows me to see those who theatrically worship, pray, and praise God simply to be seen of men. Their worship is not devoted to God but emoted to people. They run to the front of the place of worship to dance, pray, or show off their worship to God to be seen by the congregation. They only dance and praise out loud when the preacher or worship leader says the right thing. They only dance and worship if the musician hits the right note. They are acting in emotionalism and not devotionalism.

As a past worship leader and preacher, I've fallen into this category plenty of times. My devotion in worship and word started becoming a performance for the congregation and not a gift used by God or devoted to God. For a while, I stopped offering worship that would move the heart of God and offered a worship to move the crowd. My private devotion towards God became a public emotion towards people. I constantly beg God the Father to never let that be my stance again.

You don't have to pretend anymore. You don't have to put on a show for the public. Stay in private with God. Don't display yourself; let God display Himself through you. That's who you are created to be. God has created you for His good works (Eph. 2:10). You are not a sideshow attraction. Are you attracting people to you or is God using you to attract people to Him? It's time to have good character and not be a good character. It's time to cut the theatrics.

Hide-and-Seek

There was a very familiar game that I used to play with my friends when I was a kid called hide-and-seek. I don't want to assume that everyone knows this game, so let me explain how it is played. There would be a group of us that would hide from one person out of the group who would be chosen to be the finder of all of us who were hiding. I was the chosen finder or "seeker" most of the time! We would run and hide while the seeker closed his eyes or turned his back, and the seeker would count to ten and say, "Ready or not, here I come!" We would hide in the strangest place. If we were inside, we would hide in closets, cabinets, bathrooms, under the bed, or under the table just to name a few places. If we were outside, we would hide in and under cars, in trees, behind walls, and even in trash cans! I know: it's gross, but we were kids! Whoever the seeker found first would become the next seeker.

Like David, while you are hiding, the enemy is seeking you. The enemy's plan is to destroy us when he finds us. King Saul chasing David was like playing a game of hide-and-seek. King Saul sought David while David was hiding and seeking God. That should be our posture in this transformation process.

While our enemy is playing hide-and-seek towards us as the seeker, we should be in the posture of seeking God as we hide. We should be seeking His face, yielding to His commands, and hiding in His presence. We should never expose our location when the enemy is seeking us. We should be quiet and hiding so we won't be found. Too many of us are playing a game of "show-and-tell" instead of "hide-and-seek."

Allow me to explain what show-and-tell is for everyone who lived under a rock during their childhood years—just kidding—but let me explain. Show-and-tell was a segment usually during school, after school programs, or during spring and summer camp where kids would bring something valuable to them to show off to the class or camp. The kid would explain what the item meant to them and how they used the item. Kids would usually bring something sentimental given to them by a dear loved one while others bought toys, stuffed animals, and rocks. I would always bring an action figure. I remember nights that I couldn't sleep thinking about showing off my new Power Ranger gadgets and action figures.

A lot of us can't wait to show and tell the valuable things that were given to us in this process. Although it's great to be excited about our transformation in our relationship to God, it's dangerous to expose it. God wants us to move from a show-and-tell posture so that we won't expose the details and purpose of our transformation. It's dangerous for us to expose the works of God in our lives without God's permission. God is hiding you for a purpose. You can't expose it. God is using your hiding as a weapon to lure in your enemy and shift you to a higher place.

Your enemies are confused. Your spiritual adversary, the devil, is confused. You cannot be found. You are progressing by hiding. The enemy wants to end your progression, stunt your growth, and shut down your God-given purpose. The Lord has strategically hidden you so that He can lead your enemy to the appointed place of their defeat. God is deliberately hiding you in plain sight so that He can move you to new heights. The enemy does not realize that their chasing you is a strategic plan by God to chase you into your destined place. The enemy fears you, the enemy knows that you will be revealed in your destined place that God has designed for you. The enemy wants to kill before God reveals, because when God reveals, you will become the enemy's worst nightmare.

Don't give the enemy any hints to where you are. Be quiet. Study your God. Study your enemy. As your enemy plays hide-and-seek towards you, you are responsible for hiding and seeking God. Your reveal is a secret war plan ordained by God to show His great power in and through your life. Don't be an inside informant to your enemy by exposing the locations where God hides you.

Don't reveal what you've been studying. Don't reveal the jobs you're applying for. Don't reveal that you've been getting closer to God, that you are starting a business, or that you are planning to ask someone to marry you who has been sent from God, or that you have been going to the gym; that you've been working on your credit. Don't reveal the results. Because if you reveal the results to the enemy on your own, the enemy will try to kill the results. You will experience unnecessary warfare and experience delay after delay. If you let God reveal the results, the results will kill your enemy. Don't try to show results, in due time the results will show themselves. Don't explain or reveal your development, just wait for the reveal of your development.

Imagine yourself as an expectant mother and father waiting to find out the gender of their growing baby. The parents often throw a celebration for the reveal of the gender. There is an appointed time when they will find out what gender their precious baby will be, so they tell a loved one to oversee the reveal and think of a special way to reveal what the gender of the baby is. Whether it's kicking a ball full of blue powder or opening a bag full of pink balloons, the reveal is supposed to be special and meet the needs of anticipation. But what if the person planning the gender reveal party slipped up and told the parents the gender of the baby before the party? It would ruin the surprise. The anticipation of the parents would die, and they would be either disappointed or overjoyed before the celebration started. It would ruin the mood and, in some cases, would cause the parents to cancel the celebration because the surprise would be spoiled.

Your development is a surprise attack on the enemy. If you reveal your own hiding place and development, it will spoil the surprise. So, hide and seek. Seek God's face and instruction. Follow His instructions only. If He tells you to move, move! If He tells you to stay, stay! God has an appointed time to reveal your development, so that the purpose of your development can show God's power to overthrow your enemies. Don't let boredom cause you to slip and reveal yourself before God's permission has been granted. God is taking you from a place of show-and-tell, to a place of hide-and-seek. Let God show and tell; you just hide and seek.

God's Perfect Mission

In 1 Samuel chapter 23 we read about David and his troop heading into the city of Keilah. Upon his arrival the word came to David that the city was being attacked by the Philistines (1 Sam. 23:1). David inquired of the Lord and prayed whether he should attack the Philistines and defend the city of Keilah. The Lord answered David and told him to defend the city of Keilah from the hands of the Philistines, so David pursued and defeated the Philistine and took their livestock and possessions.

Let me take the time to address the importance of prayer in this transition in your life. David prayed about the opportunity to defend Keilah and waited for an answer from God before he moved. David's prayers plus God's permission produced prosperity for David and his troop. When we pray about every opportunity before we take it, we are giving God the lead to direct our paths. Whether God says yes or no, getting God's permission in prayer is vital. God's permission will give you prosperity in pursuit. God's approval releases favor in every situation and opportunity we encounter. Choosing our own path without consulting God and getting his approval to pursue our plans will cause devastating results.

In this transformation we must learn to wait for God's permission before we move or take opportunities. Moving without God's permission will turn opportunities into oppositions. The opportunities that you take that are not approved by God can be used as setups to defeat the purpose that God has for you. We must consult God and take God-ordained opportunities only, so that we won't fall into traps that we thought were regular opportunities and blessings. God's permission gives us the grace to align ourselves with God's mission, which is why I like to call God's permission God's perfect mission. God's perfect mission in the opportunities that He has allowed to be presented will be displayed in us when we communicate and commune with Him about His approval of our opportunities.

God's disapproval in prayer is vital because it will save you from utter destruction. When God says no, it's for a greater purpose. When God says no to us about an opportunity, He is actually saying no to the opportunity and not to us. God's no is an act of mercy that spares you from the dangers that are on the outside of His will. God's will and God's mission are the same thing. Prayer submits our opportunities to the goals of God. God's disapproval is God saying no to distraction and devastation. God sees setbacks before we even know that there is a possibility of setbacks. When God says "no" we night think that He hasn't answered our prayers. My friend, "no" *is* an answer, and when God says "no," He has answered. We must accept God's no and submit to the disapproval of God as we would to the approval of God.

Dr. Myles Monroe states that "Prayer is a partnership between the divine and mankind." In his sermon "Understanding the Power of Fasting," he explains that prayer is a meeting place with God. Prayer aligns our agreement with the mission of God. In prayer, we must pray for direction and confirmation of God's will in every situation. God will direct you to the right path, the path that goes in the direction of the mission that He is planning for us. Proverbs 3:5–6 states.

"Trust in the Lord with all your heart and lean not on your own understanding; in all your ways submit to him, and he will make your paths straight."

Let God Cover Your Tracks

First Samuel 23 says,

> Saul was told that David had gone to Keilah, and he said, "God has delivered him into my hands, for David has imprisoned himself by entering a town with gates and bars." And Saul called up all his forces for battle, to go down to Keilah to besiege David and his men. When David learned that Saul was plotting against him, he said to Abiathar the priest, "Bring the ephod." David said, "Lord, God of Israel, your servant has heard definitely that Saul plans to come to Keilah and destroy the town on account of me. (1 Samuel 23:7–10 NIV)

We see that David attempted to stay in the city of Keilah after he defeated the Philistines. King Saul found out that David was hiding in Keilah and sent word that he was coming to execute David while David was In

Keilah. Saul stated in verse 7 that he thought that God had delivered David into his hands as if God had given him the instruction to kill David. King Saul thought that he was doing the will of God by hunting for David's life, but King Saul confused his own insecurities with the instructions from God. King Saul's insecurity made him believe that he was doing good, when he was on a path of destruction.

It reminds me of another story of our Savior Jesus Christ the Son of God. The chief priest, elders, and teachers of the law hated Jesus and wanted to kill Him because He was liberating people from sin and giving them freedom to live without trying to keep the law. But the icing on the cake came when Jesus claimed to be the Son of God. This was blasphemous or offensive to the elders and teachers of the law. The elders, chief priest, and teachers thought they were doing well by crucifying Jesus. They didn't realize that they were crucifying Jesus out of their own self-righteous insecurity about losing control of their religion. That's why Jesus so mercifully cried out on the cross "Father, forgive them, for they do not know what they are doing" in Luke 23:34.

In 1 Samuel 23:7, King Saul was attempting to kill David from a posture of religion but not a posture of relationship. He was trying to correct his wrong on his own terms to try to please God and the Israelites. God was not with King Saul in his attempts to kill David, but God used King Saul's murder attempts to move David and his troops from one place to another. King Saul's agitation was for David's migration. David's migration was necessary for David's elevation.

David consulted God once more about Saul's approach to Keliah. David asked the Lord if Saul's attempts to find David would come to pass. The Lord spoke to David and confirmed that the King would find David in Keilah. David also asked if the citizens of Keilah would surrender David and his troops to King Saul. The Lord spoke to David and said the citizens of Keilah would surrender him and his troops to King Saul (1 Sam. 23:11–12). This caused David to gather his clan and leave before King Saul found him.

First Samuel 23 says:

> So David and his men, about six hundred in number, left Keilah and kept moving from place to place. When Saul was told that David had escaped from Keilah, he did not go there. David stayed in the wilderness strongholds and in the hills of the Desert of Ziph. Day after day Saul searched for him, but God did not give David into his hands. (1 Samuel 23:13–14 NIV)

Just like David it may sometimes seem that you are running from hiding place to hiding place trying to dodge and hide from the enemy, but God is using your running and hiding to confuse the enemy and to configure you into a new person and into a new place. God is using the chase of you to chase you into manifestation, allowing you to be chased into a higher place. While others are chasing you into their destruction, God is racing you into your destiny. All you must do is wait until God presents you. Don't present yourself. God will present what He has promised. All you must do is hide until God says that the coast is clear!

There is a strategic way that God wants you to emerge from your places of hiding. You must check your surroundings, stay quiet, move when God says move, and hide where God provides. Emerge strategically. Keep your eyes locked on the strategy that God is showing you. If you don't emerge from hiding the way that God has strategically ordered you too, it will turn the emerging into an emergency. Wait; God will reveal you in His perfect time.

Build Covenants, Not Conveniences (*Convenient* vs. *Covenant*)

First Samuel 23 records:

> While David was at Horesh in the Desert of Ziph, he learned that Saul had come out to take his life. And Saul's son Jonathan went to David at Horesh and helped him

find strength in God. "Don't be afraid," he said. "My father Saul will not lay a hand on you. You will be king over Israel, and I will be second to you. Even my father Saul knows this." The two of them made a covenant before the Lord. Then Jonathan went home, but David remained at Horesh. (1 Samuel 23:15–18 NIV)

In the middle of David's stay in Horesh, King Saul's son Jonathan sought David out to encourage and strengthen Him. David and Jonathan were best friends. Jonathan pledged his life to David's well-being. Although Jonathan's father was King Saul, Jonathan had more of a heart for David than his own power-stricken father. Jonathan committed himself to the encouragement, empowerment, and protection of his friend David. After Jonathan strengthened his friend, David and Jonathan made a covenant with each other before God and became covenant brothers. The definition of the word *covenant* is simply an "agreement, an oath, a contract." They made an oath of brotherhood before God.

In this stage of development, you don't have to find help, help will find you. God has strategic people that He has put in place to help protect and strengthen you in this run-and-hide portion of your journey. There will be people who are sent by God to encourage you, protect you, and empower you. These are the people that you must make covenants with. These are your allies. We must build strong treaties and agreements with these people because these people have a God-given heart for us. They are there for our well-being as well as our well-doing. These people are covenant people.

There's a big difference between convenient people and covenant people. The definition for *convenient* is "at hand, easily accessible." We use convenient people for company. We need covenant people for competency. Convenient people are committed to your well-doing. Covenant people are committed to your well-being. Convenient people are committed to your ideas and image. Covenant people are committed to instructions and identity. Convenient people are with you according to popularity. Covenant people are with you according to integrity.

Convenient people are all about status. Covenant people are all about support. Convenient people want you to talk more than you listen. Covenant people want you to listen more than you talk. Convenient people will only point you towards what is convenient. Covenant people will always point you to the instructions. Convenient people are seat fillers. Covenant people are place holders. Convenient people will covet you; covenant people will cover you. Conveniences waste time; covenants progress time. Don't settle for who or what is convenient. It's a trap.

Although Jonathan did not stay with David and join his clan, Jonathan's covenant with David outweighed

Jonathan's company with David. It would have been convenient for Jonathan to stay and help David fight, but Jonathan could help David a lot more by staying with King Saul as an informant who could warn David about King Saul's attempts. Jonathan did not have to fight with David to fight for David. Those in covenant with you do not always have to be with you to be for you. Convenient people are only for you when they are with you. Convenient people want to be with you so they can keep their eye on you. Covenant people keep their eye out for you and for your protection. Convenient people want to know your next move. Covenant people want to see your next move through. Those who are in covenant with you are on the lookout for you by staying close to the enemy and warning you of every move made against you.

Watch for Spies

First Samuel 23 later records the Ziphites of Ziph going to King Saul and promising King Saul that they would capture and bring David to him. David was going to The desert of Horesh in the city of Ziph. King Saul gave them his blessing.

First Samuel 23 says:

> The Ziphites went up to Saul at Gibeah and said, "Is not David hiding among us in the strongholds at Horesh, on the hill

of Hakilah, south of Jeshimon? Now, Your Majesty, come down whenever it pleases you to do so, and we will be responsible for giving him into your hands" Saul replied, "The Lord bless you for your concern for me. Go and get more information. Find out where David usually goes and who has seen him there. They tell me he is very crafty. Find out about all the hiding places he uses and come back to me with definite information. Then I will go with you; if he is in the area, I will track him down among all the clans of Judah." (1 Samuel 23:19–23 NIV)

The Ziphites were now King Saul's spies. They were responsible for gathering information about David and bringing it back to King Saul. King Saul learned about David's sneaky ways and wanted the Ziphites to get more information about David so that King Saul could track him down. King Saul told the Ziphites to get "definite information."

Watch out for spies. Spies may look like ordinary people doing ordinary activities, but they really are on a hidden mission against you for the enemy. Don't let down your guard. Don't think that you are not being watched just because you are hidden. The enemy will use inside and outside informants to track you. The convenient people that we mentioned earlier have this trait as well. Spies gather information about you to take it back to those who want to destroy you. Don't give out any unnecessary information. Beware of random questions about your whereabouts. Beware when you are asked for your opinion. Beware when you are asked to do strange activities. You may be in the eye of a spy. Be careful of those who ask a lot of questions about you but have no connection to you. You better believe that they are connected to the one who wants to destroy you. Spies will sit at your table and eat with you. They will watch you and gather as much information as they can so that they can betray you. Watch out for the Ziphites. God might be hiding you in their land, but that does not mean that they are your friends.

Let's look at the story of Samson and Delilah in Judges 16. This story reveals how the enemy will use spies to gather information about us so we can be subdued. Samson the Nazarite was the strongest man who lived at the time. Many stories in Judges speak of Samson's strength and tyranny against his enemies. Samson could take out numerous men with the jawbone of a donkey but he was weak to women. Delilah was a foreign woman and Nazarenes were forbidden to marry or be with women outside of their tribe. Samson was supposed to be living a strict Nazarite lifestyle, but Samson never kept any of the sacred vows that were made about his life as a Nazarite. One of these vows was not to sleep with foreign women, and Samson loved foreign women. Samson fell in love with Delilah. Because they were afraid of Samson, Samson's enemies, the Philistines, offered Delilah money to find out the secret to Samson's strength. She took the money and began her quest to gather information. Samson's lover became his enemy's spy.

Delilah would make love to Samson and then she would nag Samson to tell her the secret to his strength. If you are like me, you are probably wondering why Samson didn't see something wrong with his woman pressuring him to tell the secret to his strength. It seems he should have been skeptical, but Samson's guard was down. Samson was spiritually blinded by his physical delight with Delilah. Delilah constantly nagged him about the secret to his strength. Delilah tried to seize Samson's strength three times, but Samson kept lying to her about the secret of his strength. Nevertheless, Samson kept lying with the girl even after seeing that she had motives that were trying to harm his anointing, because he did not value his anointing or his vow to God.

Eventually, Delilah nagged Samson into telling her the secret, his hair. God had put the secret to Samson's strength in his hair; God flowed virtue through Samson's hair to his body. As soon as Samson told Delilah the secret to his strength, she informed her sources. She wasted no time selling him off. When Delilah informed the Philistines, they came and cut Samson's hair and poked out his eyes. They made Samson a slave, a side joke; because he was blind spiritually to his spies before he was blinded physically by his enemies. Delilah was a convenient choice and not a covenant selection. Samson lost his strength and his vision all because he refused to uphold his vows and keep his eyes on his spies. The enemy wants to take your strength and your vision by collecting information about your secrecy with God. Don't expose the secrets of God. Don't let the enemy's spies take your eyes.

Let's take another moment to peer into the life of Christ Jesus the Son of God. Jesus also had a spy for a disciple. His disciple Judas the Iscariot was used by Jesus's enemies (the elders, the chief priest, the teachers of the law, and the Pharisees) as an informant to betray Jesus. Judas walked with Christ, followed Christ, and learned from Christ just like all the other disciples. But Judas wanted money more than he wanted to stay loyal to Christ, so he made a deal with Jesus's enemies to turn Jesus over to them (Matt. 26:14–16); like the Ziphites did David and Delilah did Samson. Judas found no fault in Jesus. Judas did not have much to tell them, Judas could only show Jesus's enemies where Jesus was, and Judas betrayed Jesus by giving up His location.

Matthew 26 records:

> While he was still speaking, Judas, one of the Twelve, arrived. With him was a large crowd armed with swords and clubs, sent from the chief priests and the elders of the people. Now the betrayer had arranged a

> signal with them: "The one I kiss is the man; arrest him." Going at once to Jesus, Judas said, "Greetings, Rabbi!" and kissed him. Jesus replied, "Do what you came for, friend." (Matthew 26:47–50 NIV)

Although Judas selected convenience over covenant, Christ chose friendship over betrayal. He is merciful. Jesus kept his eye on Judas, but He allowed Judas to betray Him to fulfill the will of His Father. Jesus knew Judas would betray Him but still let Judas eat at the table. I am not telling you to dismiss your spies from your table. Let them eat with you, just don't give them the information that they are looking for. Watch and be selective about what you say. If the stories of Samson and Delilah and Jesus and Judas have taught us anything, it is this "Don't let the informant get close enough to kiss you." Watch your surroundings and watch out for spies. Don't reveal yourself without God's approval.

VII

Revenge

As we end our examination of 1 Samuel 23, we see David and his growing clan of warriors hiding from King Saul who is in hot pursuit of David's life. David is hiding in the city of Ziph, which is in the desert of Horesh, and his whereabouts were being reported back to King Saul by the Ziphites. King Saul had sent the Ziphites as spies to locate David and to tell King Saul information about David and his warriors and what they were venturing to do. When the Ziphites reported back to King Saul about David, King Saul hunted for David. David and his men removed themselves from Ziph in the Horesh desert and moved to the desert of Maon. When King Saul got word that David was Maon, he gathered his men and headed for Maon. King David arrived at the desert of Maon where David and his warriors were. David and his troop were on one side of the mountain and King Saul and his troop were on the other side. As they were attempting to approach David, a word came to King Saul from his officials that Israel was being attacked by the Philistines. This made King Saul conclude his pursuit of David and turn back to fight the Philistines.

First Samuel 23 records:

> Saul was going along one side of the mountain, and David and his men were on the other side, hurrying to get away from Saul. As Saul and his forces were closing in on David and his men to capture them, a messenger came to Saul, saying, "Come quickly! The Philistines are raiding the land." Then Saul broke off his pursuit of David and went to meet the Philistines. That is why they call this place Sela Hammahlekoth. And David went up from there and lived in the strongholds of En Gedi. (1 Samuel 23:26–29 NIV)

Now we will be journeying into 1 Samuel 24 to bring out a very vital aspect of this transformation that God is allowing to take place in your life. I will do this by explaining 1 Samuel 24 and bringing out some key points that are very important in this process of transformation from weakling to warrior.

First Samuel 24:

Revenge

After Saul returned from pursuing the Philistines, he was told, "David is in the Desert of En Gedi." So Saul took three thousand able young men from all Israel and set out to look for David and his men near the Crags of the Wild Goats. He came to the sheep pens along the way; a cave was there, and Saul went in to relieve himself. David and his men were far back in the cave. The men said, "This is the day the Lord spoke of when he said to you, 'I will give your enemy into your hands for you to deal with as you wish.'"Then David crept up unnoticed and cut off a corner of Saul's robe. Afterward, David was conscience-stricken for having cut off a corner of his robe. He said to his men, "The Lord forbid that I should do such a thing to my master, the Lord's anointed, or lay my hand on him; for he is the anointed of the Lord." With these words David sharply rebuked his men and did not allow them to attack Saul. And Saul left the cave and went his way. (1Samuel 24:1–7 NIV)

After King Saul handled the Philistines, he returned to his pursuit of David. King Saul learned that David was in the desert of En Gedi. King Saul gathered up 3,000 young troops from all of Israel and pursued David. At a certain point King Saul had to relieve himself, or as we say it in our day "use the bathroom." While King Saul was in the cave, David and his troop were in the back of the cave where King Saul was. Some of the men of David's troop reminded David of what God had said, "The men said, 'This is the day the Lord spoke of when he said to you, "I will give your enemy into your hands for you to deal with as you wish"' (1 Sam. 24:4).

This was the perfect time for David to avenge his enemy King Saul. Instead, David cut a piece of King Saul's robe without being noticed by Saul. As soon as David cut the piece of robe that King Saul was wearing, he felt convicted by God. David still honored King Saul as one of God's anointed Kings. David rebuked his troops for suggesting that he harm King Saul. King Saul relieved himself and left without harm.

Mercy Is Honor

The lesson that God showed David, the lesson that He is speaking to all of us, is about the weapon of mercy. While we are more interested in avenging our adversaries, God is more interested in reaching our adversaries by displaying mercy through us. What should've been a murder scene becomes a mercy scene with God. What should've been a scene of retaliation became a scene of rehabilitation. Retaliation precludes rehabilitation or restoration.

Revenge

Too often, we would rather destroy than restore. Pride causes us to hunger for revenge, but God wants us to tear down our pride and show mercy. David had the perfect chance to kill King Saul in the cave, but God put conviction in David's heart, so that even cutting a piece of King Saul's robe seemed like murder and not mercy to David. David was repentant about showing dishonor to God's anointed one even though David was the newly anointed king. Although David was anointed to be king, he still recognized God's anointing on King Saul's life.

Recognizing God's anointing on someone else is the gateway to displaying God's mercy. When God anoints someone, He has selected them for a special task according to His will. God has set that person to the side for His own use. Throughout the Bible God has people who were highly qualified for the task like King Saul. God has also anointed under qualified people to do a greater task just like David. The anointing of God is based on availability not qualification. Sometimes, through certain decisions they make, the anointed of God become disobedient. Even though King Saul was rejected by God as king, He was still anointed by God. David had no clue that King Saul was rejected by God; David only knew the prophet Samuel anointed him to be king. The anointing on David's life recognized the anointing on King Saul's life.

Anointing recognizes and honors anointing. The anointed are aware of the anointing on someone else's life. Honoring God's anointed demonstrates a conviction that leaves anointed people in a position to show mercy in time of retaliation. God uses the honor we show in times of retaliation as restoration to the anointed who have walked in disobedience.

First Samuel 24 reports:

> Then David went out of the cave and called out to Saul, "My lord the king!" When Saul looked behind him, David bowed down and prostrated himself with his face to the ground. He said to Saul, "Why do you listen when men say, 'David is bent on harming you'? This day you have seen with your own eyes how the Lord delivered you into my hands in the cave. Some urged me to kill you, but I spared you; I said, 'I will not lay my hand on my lord, because he is the Lord's anointed.' See, my father, look at this piece of your robe in my hand! I cut off the corner of your robe but did not kill you. See that there is nothing in my hand to indicate that I am guilty of wrongdoing or rebellion. I have not wronged you, but you are hunting me down to take my life. (1 Samuel 24:8–11 NIV)

David wanted to make it known to King Saul that he did not want to kill him, and that he honored the anointing on King Saul's life. No matter how far off King Saul was, David refused to dishonor him. David's display of God's mercy was the highest honor that He could give Saul.

First Samuel 24 continues,

> May the Lord judge between you and me. And may the Lord avenge the wrongs you have done to me, but my hand will not touch you. As the old saying goes, 'From evildoers come evil deeds,' so my hand will not touch you. "Against whom has the king of Israel come out? Who are you pursuing? A dead dog? A flea? May the Lord be our judge and decide between us. May he consider my cause, and deliver me from your hand." (1 Samuel 24:12–15 NIV)

King Saul's heart was softened so much by the mercy and honor that David had shown to him that it drove him into repentance. The mercy and honor that David walked in allowed King Saul to see his bad actions and intentions towards David. King Saul realized that God had mercy on him by showing him that his life was in David's hands to take, but David honored him instead. David allowed God's mercy to turn a place of horror into a place of honor. King Saul recognized David's anointing and assignment at that moment because he was able to look through the lens of God's mercy. King Saul was able to experience the goodness of God through the honor that David showed him, which led him to repentance (Rom. 2:4). King Saul finally admitted that David was anointed and appointed. First Samuel 24 verse 20 says "I know that you will surely be king and that the kingdom of Israel will be established in your hands." Here, King Saul acknowledged David's anointing (to be king of Israel) and his assignment (to establish the kingdom of Israel.)

The enemy is after your anointing and assignment. Your anointing represents your call from God and your assignment is the task that you are called to by God to carry out. In John 10:10 Jesus says "The thief does not come except to steal, and to kill, and to destroy. I have come that they may have life, and that they may have it more abundantly" (John 10:10 NKJV). Jesus made it clear that the thief or the enemy's job is to steal, kill, and destroy the God-given purpose that He has given us. The devil is after our anointing because, if he can kill our anointing, he can take out the bloodline and destroy our legacy and our relationship with our Creator and Savior. If the enemy can kill our assignment, he can take out the people who will be touched and who will reach beyond the borders of our legacy. These attacks are beyond you. The enemy wants the future, so he attacks the now and haunts the past. Stick to the instructions.

Rehearse the techniques. Hold fast to the promises. March forward in assurance, knowing that God will protect your anointing and your assignment as you walk in obedience to His purpose for you. God will protect your soul and direct your sword if you stay in the ordered steps that He has for you. "The steps of a good man are ordered by the Lord, / And He delights in his way" (Ps. 37:24 KJV).

The way that you keep the anointing fresh in your life is by constantly honoring the anointing on others. This is what David and his troops learned. This is spiritual wisdom, I bid that you take note as well. David showed honor and was able to have a conversation with his enemy. David's restraint bought a moment of restoration. In the Spirit, restraint is a display of strength and self-control. Although we live in a society that teaches us the opposite of this kingdom method, in the kingdom, restraint is the initiation of restoration. God will use our spiritual convictions and restraint to initiate a conversation of mercy.

The Lord God uses our convictions in the middle of our controversy to bring out conversations. The conversations are invitations to conservation, which is the prevention of wasteful use of a resource. Conservation is the act of saving or preserving something that is valuable. God's desire for His kingdom is to draw conservation from controversy. God uses our controversies as guidance for the rebellious to come to His saving grace. We are God's entryway into a situation. Coming into the kingdom of God changes our position from being an adversary into the position of an advisor who is advising our enemies to turn to God. God will literally allow you to see a moment of vengeance and restrain you so that He can show mercy to the rebellious in hopes that they will turn to Him. Our controversy is God's conversation, which represents conservation, because conservation opens the door for conversion.

First Samuel 24 records:

> When David finished saying this, Saul asked, "Is that your voice, David my son?" And he wept aloud. "You are more righteous than I," he said. "You have treated me well, but I have treated you badly. You have just now told me about the good you did to me; the Lord delivered me into your hands, but you did not kill me. When a man finds his enemy, does he let him get away unharmed? May the Lord reward you well for the way you treated me today. I know that you will surely be king and that the kingdom of Israel will be established in your hands. Now swear to me by the Lord that you will not kill off my descendants or wipe out my name from my father's family." So David gave his oath to Saul. Then Saul returned home, but David and his men went up to the stronghold. (1 Samuel 24:16–22 NIV)

King Saul recognized David's anointing that he'd been blinded to by his jealousy of David. Honor turned David's pity into piety. Honor turned King Saul's rebellion into repentance. But in his mercy, David just didn't honor King Saul, he honored God. When God convicted David's heart for cutting the robe of Saul, David repented to God and chose to honor Saul. David ran behind Saul and laid on his face. When David decided to honor and repent, it aligned his sights with God's vision about the situation. David's repentance transferred to King Saul once David aligned himself with God's intentions

My friends, a big step in this revealing process is always trying to make sure our decisions line up with mission. When we align our decision with God's mission for our situation, we unlock the grace to carry out God's vision in our lives. I'll give you this equation to follow:

Decision + Mission = Vision

Every mission that we decide to align with will birth the pieces of a bigger vision that God has ordained for our lives. Real kingdom warriors are eager to show God's intention and not their own. Real kingdom warriors who have aligned the sights of their decision with God's mission don't fight to receive the thrill of vengeance, they fight to receive the thrill of obedience. Immature warriors just want to seek vengeance. Mature warriors seek instructions so that they can remain in obedience.

Vengeance Is Mine, I Will Repay Says The Lord . . .

Let us go to Paul's letter to the Roman church where Romans 12 records:

> Repay no one evil for evil. Have regard for good things in the sight of all men. If it is possible, as much as depends on you, live peaceably with all men. Beloved, do not avenge yourselves, but rather give place to wrath; for it is written, "Vengeance is Mine, I will repay," says the Lord. Therefore "If your enemy is hungry, feed him; If he is thirsty, give him a drink; For in so doing you will heap coals of fire on his head." Do not be overcome by evil, but overcome evil with good." (Romans 12:17–21)

In this passage of scripture, Paul is addressing the church of Rome about how to conduct themselves as the church of Christ Jesus when it comes to those who have done wrong towards them. Paul referred to an ancient passage from Deuteronomy 32:35, Moses's song to Israel about the vengeance of the Lord. Paul urged the church not to avenge themselves, not to repay evil with evil, but to pray and to have mercy on enemies.

True warriors seek opportunities to show mercy to their enemies although they have every right to avenge themselves. Real warriors of the kingdom understand the difference between bringing correction and causing destruction. God did not intend for His kingdom to cause destruction but reconstruction. God wants resolution to be the first option for the kingdom. The Holy Spirit gives us the wisdom to separate the opportunities for retaliation from the opportunities for resolution. Standing against and coming against are two different actions. Coming against is the mentality of attacking an enemy. Standing against is the mentality of bringing correction to an enemy. The kingdom must stand against the forces of darkness but it must not be so quick to retaliate. We must wait for a kingdom command before we attack. If we attack without God's permission, we will hinder kingdom apprehension.

I'm reminded of Christ Jesus and His disciples at the time of His arrest. John 10 and Luke 22 record a scene of the disciple Peter cutting off the ear of the chief priest's servant. The servant's name was Malchus. I want to examine the perspective of Luke 22 on this vital story. Jesus was betrayed by Judas. Judas the Iscariot led Jesus's enemies to the Lord Jesus in the garden of Gethsemane while Jesus and the disciples were praying. When the Romans finally confirmed Jesus's identity, they attempted to lay hands on Him to arrest Him. Peter and some of the other disciples began to fight Jesus's arrestors. Peter took out his sword and sliced Malchus's right ear completely off. Look at this beautiful revelation as Jesus addressed Peter's action: "But Jesus answered, "No more of this!"

And he touched the man's ear and healed him" (Luke 22:51 NIV).

Let's go to John 18:11 to see a detailed record of what Christ said to Peter, "Jesus commanded Peter, "Put your sword away! Shall I not drink the cup the Father has given me?" (John 18:11).

Jesus knew that the disciples' retaliation hindered the Father's mission of reconciliation. The arrest, the suffering, and death were all part of God's perfect mission to reconcile humanity back into perfect fellowship with Him. Actually, Peter's retaliation worked against God's Mission in Jesus Christ.

As we mentioned before, the name of the servant of the high priest was Malchus. In Hebrew the name *Malchus* means "kingdom." The revelation of Peter cutting off Malchus's ear is that the kingdom cannot be heard if we retaliate when we are supposed to resolve. We cut off our kingdom ability to hear the instruction of God, and we cut off the kingdom from being heard when we avenge instead of avail, when we try to kill instead of heal. In verse 51 Christ healed Malchus's (the kingdom's) ear. Spiritually, Christ healed the kingdom's ability to hear and be heard.

God is not interested in your ability more than your availability. God did not make you into a warrior so that you can prove your ability to your enemies, but so you can prove your availability to Him. When you retaliate, you disqualify your availability to God so that you can show your ability to men.

Remember this: vengeance is the Lord's. We don't have the right to take revenge. We are not worthy enough. God is just, and He is the only one who can distribute justice perfectly. God will repay, we are to restore. Resolve is our job; revenge is God's job. When we take vengeance, we are trying to take God's place in the situation, and when we take vengeance, we get in God's way. When we take vengeance, we become enemies of God because in that moment we are going against His will. Vengeance is the Lord's; He will repay.

Vengeance is never justified, because we can all make the same mistakes as the person or people upon whom we are trying to wreak vengeance. God is perfect; He cannot make mistakes. His mercy is perfect, and His vengeance is perfect. Those who constantly reject the mercies of God are turned over to wickedness. Those who are deemed wicked are in line to drink from the cup of God's wrath. The sad point of all of this is that Jesus drank from the cup of God's wrath so that we don't have to, yet some still reject Him. Jesus was innocent, but He still died for the sins and crimes of mankind. Jesus is the mercy of God. But some still choose to drink from the cup of wrath. The enemies you face must encounter you, so that they can choose God's mercy or God's vengeance, but God wants everyone to choose in free will which cup they will drink from. The reason that they reject you is because they have rejected God. This powerful sermon of Jesus explains this truth. John 15 records:

> If the world hate you, ye know that it hated me before it hated you. If ye were of the world, the world would love his own: but because ye are not of the world, but I have chosen you out of the world, therefore the world hateth you. Remember the word that I said unto you, The servant is not greater than his lord. If they have persecuted me, they will also persecute you; if they have kept my saying, they will keep yours also. (John 15:18–20 KJV)

Avenging vs. Availing

See, my fellow warriors, Satan and the powers of darkness are behind every person, place, and thing that is in rebellion towards God. The Bible says in Ephesians 6:12: "For we wrestle not against flesh and blood, but against principalities, against powers, against the rulers of the darkness of this world, against spiritual wickedness in high places."

The people and places that fight against God's will in us are under the influence of the kingdom of darkness, which is ruled by Satan and his angels. We, the kingdom of God, are under the influence and control of the Holy Spirit. The Spirit of God leads to life; the spirits of darkness lead to flesh and death.

God uses our controversies as avenues of rescue for people under the control of hell's darkness. Some may choose to stay in darkness, but we must still stay available to God in our trials, so that God can make His light available through us. Jesus says in John 3:19, "This is the verdict: Light has come into the world, but people loved darkness instead of light because their deeds were evil."

We can't avenge; we must avail, so that God's perfect light will shine into the darkness.

In 1 Samuel 26, David was given the opportunity to honor King Saul by showing God's mercy instead of personal vengeance. King Saul had a second attempt of pursuing David to kill him after he and David had made an oath. There has been a bit of a time gap since the last time King Saul and David last interacted. By this time the prophet Samuel was dead and King Saul was still being tormented by his insecurity of being rejected by God almighty as king of Israel. In 1 Samuel 26 we see the Ziphites again giving information about David and his clan's location and whereabouts.

First Samuel 26:1 records: "The Ziphites went to Saul at Gibeah and said, "Is not David hiding on the hill of Hakilah, which faces Jeshimon?"

King Saul gathered up 3,000 troops and searched for David on the hill of Hakilah. Saul camped beside the wilderness of the hill of Hakilah. David and his troops were in the wilderness. David found out that King Saul was seeking to kill him again, and David did something different this time. He took one of his choice warriors named Abishai and went to face King Saul in King Saul's camp. David was used again to reveal God's perfect mission through this act. David chose to honor King Saul instead of getting revenge even though he had the advantage. He chose to honor the anointing, avail himself to God and display God's mercy although Abishai was pushing him to get revenge.

The story goes on—

First Samuel 26 says:

> So David and Abishai went to the army by night, and there was Saul, lying asleep inside the camp with his spear stuck in the ground near his head. Abner and the soldiers were lying around him.
>
> Abishai said to David, "Today God has delivered your enemy into your hands. Now let me pin him to the ground with one thrust of the spear; I won't strike him twice."
>
> But David said to Abishai, "Don't destroy him! Who can lay a hand on the Lord's

anointed and be guiltless? As surely as the Lord lives," he said, "the Lord himself will strike him, or his time will come and he will die, or he will go into battle and perish. But the Lord forbid that I should lay a hand on the Lord's anointed. Now get the spear and water jug that are near his head, and let's go." (1 Samuel 26:7–11 NIV)

David refused to strike King Saul although he had the advantage. We must learn from David to be disciplined enough to stay obedient to the convictions and instructions given by God even though we see an opportunity to avenge our own name. We must choose availability over advantage.

To have evidence of mercy, David took King Saul's water jug and spear. He left King Saul's camp and stood on the other side of the hill. While David was on the other side of the hill of Hakilah, he called for King Saul and Abner, the commander of his troops.

First Samuel 26 records:

> He called out to the army and to Abner son of Ner, "Aren't you going to answer me, Abner?" Abner replied, "Who are you who calls to the king?" David said, "You're a man, aren't you? And who is like you in Israel? Why didn't you guard your lord the

> king? Someone came to destroy your lord the king. What you have done is not good. As surely as the Lord lives, you and your men must die, because you did not guard your master, the Lord's anointed. Look around you. Where are the king's spear and water jug that were near his head?" (1 Samuel 26:14–16)

God revealed David to call out King Saul's commander and corrected him for not guarding the king. David challenged Abner's manhood. He boldly brought correction to King Saul's camp. David and his troops went from running from King Saul's camp to running through King Saul's camp. David's voice was now developed to be king. David was no longer talking, He was speaking. In human nature, talking and speaking are the same thing; in the Spirit, these two words have two different meanings. Talking is aimless, speaking is direct.

God developed David's voice in hiding. Now, he wasn't talking about his problem with King Saul, he was speaking to his problem with King Saul. Talking requires emotions; speaking requires devotion. Talking requires expressing feelings; speaking requires addressing problems. Talking is saying what you feel; speaking is saying what needs to be said. David now had the voice of the kingdom, the voice of a king. It was finally time for David to confront what he had been running from.

My friends, God is teaching us kingdom warriors how to confront the spiritual threats that we've been running from. God will produce correction from healthy confrontation. The definition of confrontation is a hostile or argumentative meeting or situation between opposing parties. God uses hostile situations to correct and bring judgment against hostility. God uses us as a vessel to confront the hostile situation to correct it. There is a much-needed conversation in the middle of confrontation. Confronting hostility strategically will turn confrontation into conversation. In God's timing, we must take on the boldness of the Holy Spirit and confront the situations and people who have chased us down. Sometimes, we even must be confrontational towards ourselves.

Don't be afraid of confrontation. Confrontation is a form of confirmation. God uses confrontation to confirm that He is confronting hostility with holiness. Don't avoid confrontation, embrace it because confrontation builds boldness. The act of confronting develops your stance and your voice. Confrontation teaches you how to stand your ground. Don't be afraid to be confrontational. Healthy confrontation can turn hostility into hospitality.

King Saul recognized David's voice as he shouted to Abner. David brings the word of the Lord to King Saul in 1 Samuel 26:

> Saul recognized David's voice and said, "Is that your voice, David my son?" David

replied, "Yes it is, my lord the king." And he added, "Why is my lord pursuing his servant? What have I done, and what wrong am I guilty of? Now let my lord the king listen to his servant's words. If the Lord has incited you against me, then may he accept an offering If, however, people have done it, may they be cursed before the Lord! They have driven me today from my share in the Lord's inheritance and have said, 'Go, serve other gods.' Now do not let my blood fall to the ground far from the presence of the Lord. The king of Israel has come out to look for a flea—as one hunts a partridge in the mountains." (1 Samuel 26:17–20 NIV)

King Saul heeded the word of the Lord from David and repented to God and David once more. King Saul vowed to not try to harm David and his troops again.

David once more used this moment not to avenge himself but to avail himself, so that the mercy of God could be shown through him.

First Samuel 26 records:

Here is the king's spear," David answered. "Let one of your young men come over and get it. The Lord rewards everyone for their righteousness and faithfulness. The Lord delivered you into my hands today, but I would not lay a hand on the Lord's anointed. As surely as I valued your life today, so may the Lord value my life and deliver me from all trouble." (1 Samuel 26:22–24 NIV)

David knew that the only one who could avenge God's anointed is God. David refused to touch God's anointed because he understood honor for the things of God. God used David's honor to elevate him and resolve the issue with Saul. God's mercy through David gave David the crown of the king who he had refused to dishonor. King Saul and David departed in peace.

Proverbs 16 records: "By mercy and truth iniquity is purged: and by the fear of the Lord men depart from evil. When a man's ways please the Lord, he maketh even his enemies to be at peace with him" (Proverbs 16:6–7 KJV).

VIII

WOUNDED WARRIORS

Kingdom warriors are dedicated to serving others. Kingdom warriors understand how essential it is to serve. Service should be the top priority for a warrior, not warfare. The definition of service is the action of helping or doing work for someone. Helping is the mentality of the kingdom. Hospitality should be at a higher standard than hostility. The weapons of the kingdom warrior are used as tools to help the kingdom and to defend the kingdom—to serve and protect—any true kingdom warrior knows that they are a servant first.

In the Sheriff's Training Academy, the first lesson we learned about the job is to "protect and serve." Service was the number one topic and the goal of the training academy. Our instructors drilled into us the importance of serving our families, our communities, and the people we worked with every day. We were taught to put our lives on the line in the name of service. We weren't taught to shoot first or how to make an arrest first. We were taught to take pride in serving before we learned anything else that we needed for the job. Protecting was subordinate to service. Serving others gave us the motivation to train to make sure that we were offering excellent service and living as servants.

Jesus is the master of all, but He still classified Himself as a servant. Jesus was not interested in being worshiped by the society around Him. He was committed to transforming the culture through servanthood and to redeeming all mankind through His sacrifice on the cross. Jesus subordinated His priesthood to servanthood. Christ desired to touch the lives of others more than He wanted to be touched. It was the will of God the Fathers that Jesus, the Messiah, descended into this fallen world as a suffering servant. The life of Christ was painted out by the prophet Isaiah in the Old Testament. Jesus's position as a lowly servant fulfilled biblical prophecy. Let us read Isaiah chapter 53, which poetically declares:

> Who has believed our message
> and to whom has the arm of the Lord
> been revealed?
> He grew up before him like a tender shoot,
> and like a root out of dry ground.
> He had no beauty or majesty to attract
> us to him,
> nothing in his appearance that we should
> desire him.

He was despised and rejected by mankind,
a man of suffering, and familiar with pain.
Like one from whom people hide their faces
he was despised, and we held him in low esteem.
Surely he took up our pain
and bore our suffering,
yet we considered him punished by God,
stricken by him, and afflicted.
But he was pierced for our transgressions,
he was crushed for our iniquities;
the punishment that brought us peace was on him,
and by his wounds we are healed.
We all, like sheep, have gone astray,
each of us has turned to our own way;
and the Lord has laid on him
the iniquity of us all.
He was oppressed and afflicted,
yet he did not open his mouth;
he was led like a lamb to the slaughter,
and as a sheep before its shearers is silent,
so he did not open his mouth.
By oppression and judgment he was taken away.
Yet who of his generation protested?

For he was cut off from the land of the living;
for the transgression of my people he was punished.
He was assigned a grave with the wicked, and with the rich in his death,
though he had done no violence,
nor was any deceit in his mouth.

Yet it was the Lord's will to crush him and cause him to suffer,
and though the Lord makes his life an offering for sin,
he will see his offspring and prolong his days,
and the will of the Lord will prosper in his hand.
After he has suffered,
he will see the light of life and be satisfied;
by his knowledge my righteous servant will justify many,
and he will bear their iniquities.
Therefore I will give him a portion among the great,
and he will divide the spoils with the strong,
because he poured out his life unto death,
and was numbered with the transgressors.
For he bore the sin of many,

and made intercession for the transgressors. (Isaiah 53:1–12 NIV)

Christ was hidden by God on purpose throughout ancient biblical scripture. Those who awaited the Messiah did not see Him appear throughout the Old Testament. Christ was hidden from their understanding because God the Father wanted to reveal Him at a specific time. Because Christ was hidden from many who thought that the prophecy in Isaiah 52 about the suffering servant was going to be fulfilled by a different person than the prophecy of the coming Messiah throughout the Old Testament as well. Christ was hidden from them until God's perfect time. Even though Jesus is Lord, Christ fulfilled the Scriptures and raised the standard of servanthood.

Christ faithfully and intensely taught the requirement of servanthood in the kingdom of God to His followers. Christ thoroughly explained that a servant was valued more than his master in the kingdom of God. God looks at those who serve as among the greatest in the kingdom. God loves a cheerful giver. People who dedicate their lives to serve others are high ranking in the kingdom. Jesus talks about who is the greatest in the kingdom of God in Matthew 18. God says whoever takes the lowly position of a child is the greatest in the kingdom. Matthew 18 records:

> At that time the disciples came to Jesus and asked, "Who, then, is the greatest in the kingdom of heaven?"
>
> He called a little child to him and placed the child among them. And he said: "Truly I tell you, unless you change and become like little children, you will never enter the kingdom of heaven. Therefore, whoever takes the lowly position of this child is the greatest in the kingdom of heaven." (Matthew 18:1–4 NIV)

The revelation of this scripture is that Jesus was talking about Himself. Jesus took off His crown of glory and left His throne to come to the world through a virgin birth and was willing to be raised as a child. Jesus was born into a world in the lowly position of a child, calling Himself the "son of man" so that He could redeem mankind and restore us back unto the Father by being born as child of God. "The Son of God became the Son of Man so that sons of man can be claimed as sons of God." —unknown

This beautiful text also speaks of creation humbling themselves as children to learn and serve in the kingdom of God. Christ humbled Himself as a child and as a servant in the earth, and He expects His believers to follow His example.

Jesus demonstrated a marvelous example of servanthood when He washed His disciples' feet in John 13, which records:

> The evening meal was in progress, and the devil had already prompted Judas, the son of Simon Iscariot, to betray Jesus. Jesus knew that the Father had put all things under his power, and that he had come from God and was returning to God; so he got up from the meal, took off his outer clothing, and wrapped a towel around his waist. After that, he poured water into a basin and began to wash his disciples' feet, drying them with the towel that was wrapped around him. He came to Simon Peter, who said to him, "Lord, are you going to wash my feet?" Jesus replied, "You do not realize now what I am doing, but later you will understand." "No," said Peter, "you shall never wash my feet." Jesus answered, "Unless I wash you, you have no part with me." "Then, Lord," Simon Peter replied, "not just my feet but my hands and my head as well!" Jesus answered, "Those who have had a bath need only to wash their feet; their whole body is clean. And you are clean, though not every one of you."

> For he knew who was going to betray him, and that was why he said not everyone was clean. When he had finished washing their feet, he put on his clothes and returned to his place. "Do you understand what I have done for you?" he asked them. "You call me 'Teacher' and 'Lord,' and rightly so, for that is what I am. Now that I, your Lord and Teacher, have washed your feet, you also should wash one another's feet. I have set you an example that you should do as I have done for you. Very truly I tell you, no servant is greater than his master, nor is a messenger greater than the one who sent him. Now that you know these things, you will be blessed if you do them. (John 13:2–17)

Christ washed His disciples' feet as a sign of servanthood; the Son of God came to show the kingdom an example of service. Christ's disciples' feet were filthy from travel and needed to be cleaned. Foot washing was considered the job of a peasant in the days of Christ. When God took off His robe and put on a servant's towel or apron and washed the disciples' filthy feet, it was the ultimate act of grace, humility, and servanthood. Jesus announced to Peter that if He did not wash Peter's feet that Peter would have no fellowship with Him. Service to others is equated to fellowship with God in the kingdom. God Almighty expects us to serve one another as He humble Himself to serve us, realizing that we were once enemies of God. That's how the kingdom works.

In Luke 22 Jesus is at the Last Supper with His disciples explaining to them the events that were about to unfold. A discussion about who is the greatest in the kingdom of God breaks out amongst the disciples at the Last Supper. Luke 22 records this exchange and Jesus's response:

> A dispute also arose among them as to which of them was considered to be greatest. Jesus said to them, "The kings of the Gentiles lord it over them; and those who exercise authority over them call themselves Benefactors. But you are not to be like that. Instead, the greatest among you should be like the youngest, and the one who rules like the one who serves. For who is greater, the one who is at the table or the one who serves? Is it not the one who is at the table? But I am among you as one who serves. (Luke 22:24–27 NIV)

This account is parallel to the one in Matthew 18. The servant is the greatest in the kingdom of God. Those who serve are considered mighty in God's eyes. Service is a special gift and a weapon given to the kingdom of God in the earth to spread God's goodness throughout the earth in Jesus's name.

Jesus announces His position as a servant in Matthew 20:28 and Mark 10:45. Proclaiming in both accounts "just as the Son of Man did not come to be served, but to serve, and to give his life as a ransom for many." Christ was showing His humility to serve as a suffering servant that was promised, even though He is the Great Messiah of Israel, to restore the nation back unto God that was promised as well. Both problems are one promise. Christ came as the suffering servant and gave His life so that we can be called back into right standing with God. Christ rose from the dead and concreted the example of servanthood to mankind. Servanthood is how the Messiah wants His kingdom to operate, so service had to be displayed by Him as a suffering servant. Christ's life beautifully announces, Do as I say *and* do as I do.

No longer Servants, but friends

When we dedicate our lives to service in the kingdom, God takes us personally. We are not just creation through Christ, we are God's children through Christ. Our birth on earth identifies us as God's creation, our birth in Christ places us as God's children. When we dedicate our lives to service, God calls us close to see secrets that we would have never seen from the outside looking in. Kingdom warriors are servants who dedicate their lives to service so they can serve God from the inside out and not from the outside in. God has a personal relationship with those who serve and walk closely with Him. God not only calls us servants, but He also calls us friends.

John 15 records: "I no longer call you servants because a servant does not know his master's business. Instead, I have called you friends, for everything that I learned from my Father I have made known to you" (John 15:15 NIV).

When we dedicate our lives to the Father's business, which is His kingdom, God calls us His friends and begins to reveal instructions and mysteries to us. The Lord trusts those who serve in His name. Serving in the kingdom goes beyond serving in the local church, although that is important as well. Serving in the kingdom is a daily life committed to serving others and being obedient to the instructions that the Spirit of God gives you to do. A friend serves. God serves His friends, and He expects His friends to dedicate themselves to servanthood.

Open Wounds

I know that some of the readers of this book may be thinking, *How does being a servant relate with being a wounded warrior?* Allow me to sow the topic together for you. When Christ ascended to heaven to prepare a place for His followers, He gave us a command to serve each other as if He were walking the earth. When we serve each other in the kingdom, Christ takes it personal—as if you are doing it for Him.

In Matthew 25 Jesus says,

> I was naked and you clothed me, I was sick and you visited me, I was in prison and you came to me. "Then the righteous will answer him, saying, 'Lord, when did we see you hungry and feed you, or thirsty and give you drink? Or when did we see you as a stranger and welcome you, or naked and clothe you? And when did we see you sick or in prison and visit you?' And the King will answer them, 'Truly, I say to you, as you did it to one of the least of these my brothers, you did it to me.' (Matthew 25:36–40 ESV)

Christ our commander is very serious about us serving one another. Sometimes service puts us in the position to be taken advantage of. Just as Christ served those who would later order Him to be crucified. We will run into people who will abuse our servanthood, but Christ still expects us to serve.

Our gifts to service the kingdom of God and to bring the kingdom of God to the earth were given to us by the Holy Spirit. The Bible says that our gifts have been given to us to edify the body of Christ and to glorify the Father in heaven (1 Corinthians 14:12; James 1:7). When we humble our gifts for kingdom use, we draw people to the glory of God. God uses our gifts through servanthood to serve the need of the kingdom of God on the earth.

There's a difference between serving a need and serving a want. One is servanthood and one is prostitution. A servant who is used for personal gain is considered a prostitute. Service that's taken advantage of is prostitution. Prostitution is the unworthy or corrupt use of one's talents for the sake of personal or financial gain. Service can become prostitution when you don't take the time to learn the value of your gift and service. When you don't know your gift's value, you will give it away cheaply. People love bargains, but your service is not a bargain, it's a valuable gift from God. We give away sacred things because of our lack of wisdom about the value in the kingdom. The Holy Spirit will give us wisdom in service so that we will not be prostituted.

Valuable places attract vulnerable people, Valuable people are attracted to vulnerable places because they see an opportunity to take advantage of the opportunities in vulnerable places. They look for places to upgrade. Vulnerable people are attracted to valuable places because they see an opportunity to gain value without doing the work of what's valued. Some take advantage of the value of a servant, but they don't take care of the servant because of their vulnerabilities in the earth.

Many servants have been spiritually raped by the ones that they've served or are serving under. The abuse has caused wounds that seem unhealable. So many top kingdom warrior servants have broken confidence because they were spiritually traumatized by masters or commanders who mishandled them. Many warriors have been wounded and put out of commission from kingdom ventures because their wounds are still open and bleeding. Many top kingdom servants or warriors are still shattered from the abuse. They have lost the confidence to stand and serve because of the embarrassment and shame caused by masters who don't have servant's hearts.

Sometimes, servants are abused in the earth because their master or leader wants the gift that the servant holds but they throw the servant away. Servants are sometimes merchandised instead of utilized. When a master treats a servant like property and not a helping hand, abuse is inevitable. That's because some who are called to be a master or to be in charge for a season, are not servants themselves. They are motivated by their own personal gain. A master who is not a servant is considered a merchant. A person who serves under a servant will be exalted. A person who serves under someone who is a merchant will be exploited. God sent judgment to this certain type of masters or shepherds in the book of Jeremiah. God was addressing some of the leaders of Israel during this prophecy, but the lesson applies to us spiritually.

Jeremiah 23:1–4 (NIV) records:

"Woe to the shepherds who are destroying and scattering the sheep of my pasture!" declares the Lord. 2 Therefore this is what the Lord, the God of Israel, says to the shepherds who tend my people: "Because you have scattered my flock and driven them away and have not bestowed care on them, I will bestow punishment on you for the evil you have done," declares the Lord. 3 "I myself will gather the remnant of my flock out of all the countries where I have driven them and will bring them back to their pasture, where they will be fruitful and increase in number. 4 I will place shepherds over them who will tend them, and they will no longer be afraid or terrified, nor will any be missing," declares the Lord.

Healing for Kingdom Warriors

Allow me to act as your doctor at this moment. Untreated open wounds cause infection. The longer that infection goes untreated, the wider the infection will spread. Many wounded servants or warriors are bleeding. They have open, infected wounds and, as time goes by, they become heavily infected because of the lack of treatment. The lack of treatment causes toxins to be released throughout the whole body, infecting the whole body with all types of sicknesses. One wound can affect your mind, body, and soul. Infected, open wounds cause better servants to become bitter servants. Bitterness untreated always grows into wickedness, which causes rebellion against God.

Rabies is a viral disease that originates from an Australian bat that infects humans and animals. Rabies is caused by animal bites. After an animal with rabies bites a human or another animal, the saliva from the bite infects the human or animal causing inflammation of the brain and other deadly effects. The bite penetrates the skin and introduces the disease through the person or animal's bloodstream. Some animals that have been bitten display unusual, aggressive, and erratic behavior. The infection causes some animals to become aggressive and bite others for no expected reason. Both animals and humans with untreated rabies infections can suffer deadly results.

When spiritual wounds are left untreated they can also affect the body. Once wounds have become infected in one part of the body of Christ, the infection spreads to the rest of the body. Some spiritually wounded people behave just like animals with rabies and bite others for no expected reason. They go around biting and infecting others, inflicting wounds because of the bitterness of their own infection. The wounds begin to operate in the body. Fighting, slander, rage, isolation, depression, and distrust are all signs of infected spiritual wounds. A person must get treatment, or the infection will take over. I will explain later in this chapter what treatment consists of.

Many kingdom warriors were not wounded by their own leaders, but they were wounded by other leaders they had been sent to serve by their own leaders, whom they'd been sent to serve and to lend a hand. Some were sent as representatives and returned wounded because they were mishandled on the assignment by the people they were sent to serve. I'm talking to those who have received harsh treatment that they did not deserve because they were just doing as they were told, those who were hurt while being obedient. There is an account in the Old Testament that describes this type of situation. Let's journey back to David and his troop for a moment. The story is in 2 Samuel 10. Instead of reciting all the scripture, I will give you a brief about the story and show how it relates to wounded warriors.

It is very important for us to know that David is now King David of Israel in this specific text. King David has taken the place of his master and oppressor King Saul. King Saul has been dead for a while at this point in the story (1 Sam. 31). King David was faithful over the troop that he was given and now God has given Him a kingdom to run. King David has been on many military exploits and campaigns by this time. King David has also made a lot of mistakes. We've seen King David's growth as a servant, a warrior, and a leader as we read 1 and 2 Samuel.

Second Samuel 10 and 1 Chronicles 19 tell a story about King David's attempt to show kindness to Hanun, the son of King Nahash of Ammon. King Nahash had died; David sent some of his warriors to send condolences to Hanun who was now King since his Father Nahash's death. King David sent his servants to serve and be kind to Hanun because King Nahash had shown David kindness during his reign. Scripture doesn't document what King Nahash did that King David considered as kindness, but King David was convinced that He needed to keep the kindness and friendship going with Nahash's son Hanun. When King David's servants arrived in Ammon, the officials falsely accused King David's servants of being spies.

Second Samuel 10 records: "[T]he Ammonite officials said to their lord Hanun, 'Do you really think David is trying to honor your father by sending these messengers to express his sympathy? No, David has sent his servants to you to get information about the city and spy on it so they can overthrow it!" (2 Samuel 10:3 NET).

King David sent his servants to Ammon with good intention, but his attempts to show kindness were responded to with assault. King David was insulted while his servants were assaulted. King David's servants were just being obedient to their master's commands, and they were attacked for it, which wasn't fair. Second Samuel 10:4 (NET) records: "So Hanun seized David's servants and shaved off half of each one's beard. He cut the lower part of their robes off so that their buttocks were exposed, and then sent them away."

Hanun responded to King David's kindness with assault. Hanun did two things to King David's servants that are very significant in terms of how servants or warriors are really wounded. Hanun shaved off half of their beards and cut off the back half of their robes, exposing their backsides. How humiliating. The servants returned to King David humiliated, vulnerable, and broken. They were wounded spiritually. I want to explain what these two assaults mean spiritually in explaining the wounds of warriors.

1.) Half shaven beards:

In the Israelite culture for a man to shave his beard was a symbol of disgrace. Shaving half of King David's servants' beards was a symbol of dishonor from Hanun to King David and a symbol of emasculation for King David's servants. Spiritually, the half shaven beards represent broken confidence in identity. The servants lost their identity when their beards were shaved. To have to walk around with half a beard was emasculating. To be taken advantage of for your service when you came in good will is humiliating. Hanun snatched their identities from them, and they walked away in shame. They were innocent but suffered a great embarrassment at the hands of those they were sent to serve.

If you are a spiritually wounded kingdom warrior, what has shaved away your identity? What happened to make you lose your identity? What stole your confidence in who God called you to be? Who shaved your beard? Who took your kindness and used it against you? Who trashed your influence? What made you lose confidence in what God sent you to do? What act made you unrecognizable?

2.) Half cut robes:

Hanun cut the robes of King David's servants as an act of disrespect directly from Hanun to King David. This act was an act of exposure and spiritually signified the broken confidence in their covering. Hanun cut their robes exposing their buttocks and private parts. This act was done to break their confidence in covering, to make their covering appear weak. The goal was to make the servants of King David lose confidence in his judgment. They would question why King David would send them to serve such a tyrant and lose confidence in his covering ability.

I have more spiritual questions for you. Who cut your robe? What made you start distrusting those who guide you? What made you stop attempting to seek counsel? What made you fearful in your obedience? Who exposed your private parts while you were just trying to be obedient? What and who broke your confidence in your covering? I challenge you to write these questions down and let the Holy Spirit answer them so you can properly heal.

David's servants' beards were shaven and their garments were cut. The beard represented confidence in identity and the robe represented confidence in covering, both of which were cut in half. These servants came back to King David humiliated, ashamed, and unconfident. King David was highly disrespected and felt the pain of his servants, who were just being obedient to him. King David gave them methods of healing that I want us to dig into and apply to our lives as warriors if we are ever wounded.

Second Samuel 10:5 (NET) records: "Messengers told David what had happened, so he sent them to the men who were thoroughly humiliated. The king said, 'Stay in Jericho until your beards have grown again; then you may come back.'"

There are three things that King David told his servants to do that I want us to break down step-by-step.

1.) Stay in Jericho

King David told his messenger to tell his servants to stay in Jericho in the state that they were in. Jericho was in the middle of the journey back home for King David's servants. King David's servants had already walked half the journey naked, afraid, and ashamed. King David sent his messenger to where they were to tell them to stay put and not try to come home in the condition that they were in.

The spiritual wisdom behind this instruction from King David to his servant is "Stay still and heal." Many of us are wounded and leaking trails of blood behind us because we refuse to stay still, because we are fearful of staying still. We are fearful of dying in the state that we are in, so we keep moving to stay alive. We feel like movement will keep us distracted from devastation. We are fearful of what might happen to us if we finally deal with the wounds we carry. Sometimes busyness is a distraction from healing, but busyness does not always mean progress. We refuse to stay still and heal. When we have been spiritually wounded, we must learn to back into the secret place with God, stay still, and let Him heal us. We should not try to operate in our gifts if we have open wounds. We should address the wounds first so that we can properly serve with a pure heart and intentions.

When someone breaks a bone, medical staff immobilize the bone by putting the arm, leg or whatever bone is broken into a cast or splint to eliminate as much movement as possible. The bone must be still so it can be healed. Too much movement can injure the bone more to the point where it is unhealable. The abnormality becomes a deformity when the injury or break doesn't heal properly. Stillness is the proper method of healing. Don't do a lot of talking, especially about what wounded you. Don't be on the scene until your healing has taken place. Don't move until you are completely healed. Step back, rest, stay still, and heal.

2.) Let your beard grow again

It was important for King David to instruct them to stay in Jericho until their beards had grown back as a sign of restoration. To a man in King David's time and culture, the beard was a sign of confidence and identity. A nice beard was a sign of covenant, and to the Israelite man this was a sign of devotion. This came from one of the laws that God gave to Moses for the Israelites to follow in Leviticus. Leviticus 19:27 (NIV) records: "Do not cut the hair at the sides of your head or clip off the edges of your beard."

For the beards of the servants to be half shaven was a total disgrace to their beliefs, culture, and to their manhood. David ordered the men to remain in Jericho until their beards grew again. The spiritual wisdom behind this instruction is to grow confidence in who you are again. Confidence takes root in the soul like the roots of trees in dirt or the follicles of hair in skin. Just like a beard that is plucked, confidence is painful when it is plucked from the soul. Plucked confidence leaves the soul bleeding like a scalp that hair has been ripped from.

Staying in Jericho until your beard grows back is spiritually equivalent to saying, "Stay still until confidence grows again." You must learn who you are again. You must take time to study who you are in Christ again and who you are becoming. You must seek counseling, read, pray, fast, and rest so that you will be filled with the confidence that God wants you to have to be a kingdom warrior and servant.

You also must forgive. Forgiveness is vital in healing. You must forgive the crime and sin done against you and learn from the experience that's behind you. Forgive the person and the situation. If you can't forgive, you will become a slave to the one or ones who humiliated you. Whether male or female, you need confidence to do what God has called you to do. We must completely let go and forgive our trespassers so that our beards or our confidence in who God is and who we are in God can grow stronger and longer than before. It's time for your beard to grow again, it's time for your confidence to heal.

3.) Come back

King David instructed his servants to "Stay in Jericho until your beards have grown again; then you may come back." King David instructed them to heal and grow before they came back home. King David knew that the servants were trying to make it home, so he ordered them to stay and completely heal before returning. King David also instructed them to come back.

The spiritual wisdom for this instruction is to return to service. After being healed from something that was traumatic to our hearts and souls, we sometimes get comfortable and decide to stay put in a place that God used for our healing. We become complacent and comfortable in Jericho, but we are called to return after we are healed and whole. We must make sure we learn from the last situation and apply it to our lives.

Coming back doesn't mean going back to what used to be. King David didn't tell them to return to Hanun; he told them to return home. Even in their humiliation, King David still needed their service. King David needed His servants healed up and ready to serve before returning home. He ordered them to return after their confidence, strength, and identity had been restored.

I want to tell you the same thing. Coming back doesn't mean going back to a bad situation, unless God's Spirit tells you to. Coming back spiritually means continuing to serve. Although you have been hurt, humiliated, and disrespected, don't let those things rape you of your posture of servanthood. Don't deny servanthood because of those who chose to take advantage of you. Your service is still needed; God still wants to use your gift. Most of all, God still loves and wants *you*. Even though you feel worthless, your life has purpose. God wants you to be healed mind, body, and spirit. Stay still, let your confidence grow, and don't forget to return to service when you are healed.

This cruel story of the humiliation of King David's servants is a beautiful reality about the coming of the Lord Jesus Christ. Jesus went through everything on the day of His arrest, trial, and death that these suffering servants went through while on assignment for King David. This story of their mistreatment was a shadow of the abuse and mistreatment of Christ. Let's dig deeper into an Old Testament prophecy about Christ and see how it compares to this story and the story of the reality of Jesus as a suffering servant.

Isaiah 50 says,

The Sovereign Lord has given me a well-instructed tongue, to know the word that sustains the weary. He wakens me morning by morning, wakens my ear to listen like one being instructed.

The Sovereign Lord has opened my ears; I have not been rebellious,

I have not turned away.

I offered my back to those who beat me, my cheeks to those who pulled out my beard;

I did not hide my face from mocking and spitting.

Because the Sovereign Lord helps me, I will not be disgraced.

Therefore have I set my face like flint, and I know I will not be put to shame. (Isaiah 50:5–7 NIV author's paraphrase)

This book of Isaiah is known to have the most prophecies about Jesus Christ's suffering in the Old Testament. This song of prophecy by Isaiah mirrors the story of King David's suffering servants and Jesus Christ's betrayal, arrest, and crucifixion. Let's look closely at the verses that relate to Jesus.

> Verse 4: "The Sovereign Lord has given me a well-instructed tongue, to know the word that sustains the weary. He wakens me morning by morning, wakens my ear to listen like one being instructed."

Jesus is the Word of God (John 1) sent by His Father in heaven and instructed to restore a fallen world back unto Him through love, power, and sacrifice. Jesus followed His Father's instruction perfectly. Christ's whole life was about doing what God the Father sent Him to do (Isa. 55:11).

> Verse 5: "The Sovereign Lord has opened my ears; I have not been rebellious; I have not turned away."

Jesus was completely obedient to the law. He followed it perfectly, and there was and is no fault or sin found in Him. In Matthew 4, Jesus was tempted on every hand with the same temptations that Adam, Eve, and all of mankind had fallen to and rebelled against God. Christ never sinned but still took the punishment.

> Verse 6: "I offered my back to those who beat me, my cheeks to those who pulled out my beard; I did not hide my face from mocking and spitting."

This verse resembles the suffering servants of King David in 2 Samuel and 1 Chronicles. Christ allowed Himself to be arrested, humiliated, beaten, scorned, have His beard plucked from his face, and whipped so brutally that He was unrecognizable (Isa. 52:14).

The humiliation, the disrespect, and the shame He faced as He offered Himself as a ransom to those who took His sacrifice as blasphemy to God but didn't realize that He was the Son of God who had been promised.

> Verse 7: "Because the Sovereign Lord helps me, I will not be disgraced. Therefore have I set my face like flint, and I know I will not be put to shame."

This lovely prophecy was fulfilled and its fulfillment is described in the New Testament in Hebrews 12:2 (NIV), which says, "fixing our eyes on Jesus, the pioneer and perfecter of faith. For the joy set before him he endured the cross, scorning its shame, and sat down at the right hand of the throne of God."

Christ displayed the ultimate life of servanthood. He laid down His life and His will to come to earth to redeem a fallen world. He forgave those who bargained for His crucifixion and death. He came to show the love and heart of the Father just as He was instructed to do and those that He came to save in His Father's name chose to put Him to death. But Jesus gave forgiveness to those who crucified Him crying to God the Father, "Father, forgive them, for they do not know what they are doing" as they divided up his clothes (Luke 23:34 NIV). They ripped His clothes, plucked His beard, and taunted Him. Jesus yielded His will to the Father to drink the bitter cup of His Father's wrath that was meant for those who are enemies of God (Matt. 26:39; John 19:28–39). His only mission was to do the will of the Father and to destroy the works of the devil. He gave up His life and stayed still in a grave for three days. But Jesus didn't stay still for long. He rose again in a glorified body in confidence. Now, to spread His life throughout the earth through His servants and friends, we who are His children, servants, friends, and warriors should live as He lived and lives. Jesus, the Lord of heaven's armies, became the wounded warrior on earth so that our wounds can be healed and we can again be whole warriors. He was wounded for our wounds; His wounds heal our wounds.

Jeremiah 30:17 records: "But I will restore you to health, and heal your wounds, declares the Lord, 'because you are called an outcast, Zion for whom no one cares'" (Jer. 30:17 NIV).

The healing in a warrior's faith

It takes faith to be healed. No matter how bloody and deep your wound is, you will have the faith to recover when you have true faith in God. Faith is complete trust or confidence in someone or something. You must have faith in the Lord for the instructions He has given to you in this healing process (Rom. 10:17). If you don't have complete confidence in God, you will not have the confidence to take the steps of healing that are necessary for your recovery.

Hebrews 11:6 (NIV) records: "And without faith it is impossible to please God, because anyone who comes to him must believe that he exists and that he rewards those who earnestly seek him."

Even in our despair we must have the faith to earnestly seek the Lord. As we seek the Lord, healing will take place. The faith we hold in Christ Jesus alone releases healing and restoration to us as we earnestly seek to trust and serve the Lord. There is power when warriors or servants release their faith even though they are in a bad state. Christ will heal whatever we are willing to reveal to Him. It takes faith to reveal a wound to the Lord. It also takes faith for the Lord to heal whatever we reveal to Him (James 1:6–7). When we come to God with our wounds in confidence, God will reward us with healing because we have complete confidence in Him. Our faith moves God.

It also takes faith to sit back and rest. I know you are used to moving. God has ordered you to sit, rest, and heal. You must trust God when He calls for you to rest. It's for your own good. All warriors need rest. When you constantly move when God says rest, you are being disobedient, and you are not putting faith in God. Have faith in God's instruction to rest and heal.

There's a beautiful account in the gospel of Matthew chapter 8 verses 5 through 15 about a Roman Centurion who came to Jesus in faith for the healing of his servant who was paralyzed. A centurion is the commander of a century or a company of one hundred men in the ancient Roman army. The centurion was a powerful commander who humbly came to Jesus in faith asking for his servant to be healed.

Jesus offered to come to the Centurion's house to see about his servant, but the centurion forbids Jesus because he did not feel worthy enough to have Jesus in his home. Verses 8 and 9 record their exchange: "The centurion replied, 'Lord, I do not deserve to have you come under my roof. But just say the word, and my servant will be healed. For I myself am a man under authority, with soldiers under me. I tell this one, 'Go,' and he goes; and that one, 'Come,' and he comes. I say to my servant, 'Do this,' and he does it."

Christ was astonished by the centurion's faith, stating that He had not found such great faith in all of Israel. Christ was moved by the faith of the centurion, and He met the centurion's request and sent him back home. When the centurion arrived home, his servant was healed.

The beautiful revelation in this passage of scripture is that God honored the commander's request when he humble himself as a servant of Christ. The centurion was a powerful man with servants and soldiers but he felt powerless and humbled himself in reverence to Christ. The centurion realized that no matter how powerful he was on earth, he did not have the power to heal his servant. He humbled himself as a servant to Jesus and asked that his servant be healed. This took faith. The centurion was a Roman, not an Israelite. The roman centurion had to cast aside all that he was and knew to come before Jesus. The master had to become a servant so that healing could flow through his faith. The centurion's faith was an avenue of healing for his servant. All the servant has to do is rest and wait for healing. The centurion's faith met Jesus and Jesus met the need.

The faith of a warrior will always display the heart of a servant. It takes faith to cast your position aside to recognize that God has true power and only He can heal the things that are concerning us. When warriors display a servant's faith, healing takes place.

Wounds vs. Scars

Jesus told Peter at the Last Supper that Peter would deny Him. Just before telling Peter about His denial, Jesus told Peter about the devil's plot to attack his faith. Luke 22:31–32 (NIV) records Jesus's words: "Simon, Simon, Satan has asked to sift all of you as wheat. But I have prayed for you, Simon, that your faith may not fail. And when you have turned back, strengthen your brothers."

Jesus supplied restoration for Peter even before Peter's faith was damaged. Denying Christ wounded Peter because Peter loved Jesus, but because Peter was a human filled with sin, he failed. Jesus already supplied healing to Peter and his faith before the denial took place. Jesus commanded that after Peter had repented and come back, that he was instructed to strengthen his brothers and fellow disciples. After Peter denied Christ, Peter's faith was shattered. Peter hid himself, went back to fishing, drinking, and living his old lifestyle. When Christ rose from the dead, He spoke to Peter while they were eating together and drew Peter back into fellowship (John 21:14–16). Peter returned with a testimony of the grace of Christ as a scar of the love of God. Christ turned Peter's apostasy into apostleship. Christ turned the wound of denial into a scar of restoration. In faith, Peter returned and preached the gospel of Christ with the testimony of God's love and grace which was used to keep his fellow brothers and to attract future believers of Christ into the grace of Christ.

Warriors, let your faith reach out for your healing. Don't stay wounded. Let your wounds heal into scars. Wounds turn into scars when healing is applied. Scars are a testimony that healing can take place. Your wounds will turn people away, but your scars will attract people to your healing and to what healed you. Christ already has the treatment for your wound available. Your faith must grab the healing. Release your faith in God's instructions that will lead to your healing. When you are healed, testimony will be revealed.

Final Words

The problems of transformation presented in this book—

1.) When you are troubled, lost, and need guidance:

2.) When weaknesses try to become your identity:

3.) When God hides you in isolation to develop you:

4.) When your weaknesses cause you to be ashamed:

5.) When you are learning how to stand against what or who makes you weak:

6.) When you feel like you are ready to face your enemies and your problems after you've been strengthened:

7.) When you want to take vengeance on your enemies after you have been strengthened:

8.) When you are dealing with wounds from serving others:

The Solutions we have learned from this book:

1.) Seek for discipleship; submit to the teacher God has led you to.

2.) Allow your weaknesses to be addressed.

3.) Remain hidden in the secret place with the Lord.

4.) Embrace the discipline that comes with embarrassment.

5.) Submit to the wisdom of warfare.

6.) Don't come out of hiding without God's permission and strategy.

7.) Focus on instructions, be merciful, and leave vengeance to God.

8.) Let God heal your wounds and return you to service.

This Is a Call to All Kingdom Warriors:

It's time to rise and stand against the kingdom of darkness. Weaknesses are not supposed to become our identity; they are supposed to be an entry point for God to use us in His glorious grace. Your weakness was allowed by God so that you and those who encounter you can have a testimony of God's great strength. There are many more steps that God has given me in this process of transformation that the Lord is manifesting in our lives, but God specifically instructed me to give these eight instructions as the initiation as a kingdom warrior. These steps are fundamental, educational, and vital in this process of transformation.

It is creation's instinct to sin and rebel against God. Because of the curse caused by Adam and Eve's disobedience, all of us fall short of the glory of God (Rom. 3:23). God must reprogram our minds to put His instructions over instinct. The mindset of David, of the 400, or any other biblical reference used to describe a weak person tasked to do God's will has to stand strongly against instinctive thoughts, words, and behaviors.

The word that weaves this whole book together is *mentality*. God is grooming our mentalities away from the systems of this world and into the mentality of His kingdom. Mentality is the characteristic attitude of mind or way of thinking of a person or group. If God can transform our mentality to think and function the way He intends for our mentality to function, we will be able to do many great kingdom exploits without the limitations that the mind and the flesh put on us on earth. Apostle Paul writes in Romans 12:2, "And be not conformed to this world: but be ye transformed by the renewing of your mind, that ye may prove what is that good, and acceptable, and perfect, will of God."

When we allow our minds to be renewed in Christ Jesus, we will be transformed to do the perfect will of the Father. The will of the Father is displayed in Christ Jesus and through the church, the kingdom of God. Jesus inaugurated the kingdom of God in His first coming as the servant who was sacrificed. He came as the Lamb of God. In His second coming Christ will return with His kingdom to establish His kingdom on earth and destroy wickedness once and for all. Christ will establish a new heaven and earth (Rev. 21:1–2). Christ is giving us the mind or mentality of His kingdom movement and establishment.

Our mentalities must be transformed to the mind of Christ to be effective kingdom servants and warriors. Mental healing takes place where mental transformation is embraced. We are to set our minds on the kingdom of God that is to soon be established and stand against the kingdom of darkness. We have been resurrected with Christ, to die to the deeds of the flesh and to embrace the life God has given us in Christ Jesus for the kingdom of God. Paul writes in Colossians 3:

If then you have been raised with Christ, keep looking for the good things of heaven. This is where Christ is seated on the right side of God. Keep your minds thinking about things in heaven. Do not think about things on the earth. You are dead to the things of this world. Your new life is now hidden in God through Christ. Christ is our life. When He comes again, you will also be with Him to share His shining-greatness. (Colossians 3:1–4 NLV)

In Philippians 2 Paul writes about the mind that we should embrace if we are in Christ and are to represent the kingdom of God. He instructs us:

Let this mind be in you, which was also in Christ Jesus: Who, being in the form of God, thought it not robbery to be equal with God: But made himself of no reputation, and took upon him the form of a servant, and was made in the likeness of men: And being found in fashion as a man, he humbled himself, and became obedient unto death, even the death of the cross. Wherefore God also hath highly exalted him, and given him a name which is above every name:0 That at the name of Jesus every knee should bow, of things in heaven, and things in earth, and things under the earth;1 And that every tongue should confess that Jesus Christ is Lord, to the glory of God the Father. (Philippians 2:5–11 NKJV)

When we exalt Christ's instruction above our earthly instincts, manifestation of God's promises will be frequent in our lives. When we seek the kingdom first, manifestation is inevitable. The kingdom will always hold evidence.

When we stop seeking for our own pleasure and seek for the things that please the Lord, God will add whatever we need for the life that He has called us to. Jesus says in Matthew 6,

So do not worry, saying, 'What shall we eat?' or 'What shall we drink?' or 'What shall we wear?' For the pagans run after all these things, and your heavenly Father knows that you need them. But seek first his kingdom and his righteousness, and all these things will be given to you as well." (Matthew 6:31–33 NIV)

It's time for you to embrace the kingdom warrior that God has called you to be. You and I are tasked with following our Lord's instruction so that we can cause an impact for God's Kingdom in the earth in our time. But first we must allow God to enter our weaknesses and show His mighty strength through us. In Ephesians 6:10 (NIV), the apostle Paul records: "Finally, be strong in the Lord and in his mighty power."

Let God transform your weaknesses into a canvas to display His strength and then you can live as the warrior that God has called and transformed you to be in every area of your life. Warriors, arise! It's time to let go of the weakling that you were and embrace the warrior that you are! Trust in the Lord God who specializes at transforming weaklings into warriors!

Hebrews 4 commands:

Therefore, since we have a great high priest who has ascended into heaven, Jesus the Son of God, let us hold firmly to the faith we profess. For we do not have a high priest who is unable to empathize with our weaknesses, but we have one who has been tempted in every way, just as we are—yet he did not sin. Let us then approach God's throne of grace with confidence, so that we may receive mercy and find grace to help us in our time of need. (Hebrews 4:14–16 NIV)

Acknowledgments

I want to thank My Lord and Saviour Christ Jesus for this opportunity. I count it as a privilege to partner with the Lord in the writing of this book. I love you Lord. Thank you for being my Father, Friend and my Everything. I also want to thank my beautiful wife Queen and our beautiful children Ezra, Essence, Kollyn and Cyrus. I love you all so much. Thank you for your wonderful love and endless support. Thank you to Prophet Richard Rowe for your intense prophetic counsel and brotherhood. It has truly changed my life. Thank you to everyone, family and friends for your love and support! God bless you all!

About the Author

Terence S. Benton is a devout follower of Christ and Kingdom enthusiast. Born in 1993 in Portsmouth, Virginia, **Terence S. Benton** began working in worship and youth ministry as a young teenager. Terence has been an enthusiast for the Kingdom of God for almost 15 years and has expanded his experience into the Law Enforcement and Education fields. **Terence S. Benton** is the husband of one beautiful wife and the father of 4 beautiful children. **Terence S. Benton** is a writer, poet, songwriter, composer, minister, worship leader, educator and new author. Now based in Arlington, Texas, Terence will continue to follow the Spirit of God, love his family , love people, write and expand the Kingdom of God for the rest of his life.

CPSIA information can be obtained
at www.ICGtesting.com
Printed in the USA
LVHW052127171022
730903LV00004B/202